Capitalism Doesn't Fail

By

Robert Villegas

Capitalism Doesn't Fail
By Robert Villegas

© Copyright 2019 by Robert Villegas.
© Copyright 2020 by Robert Villegas.
No part of this book may be reproduced in any manner without the express written agreement of the author and his designated legal authority. All Rights Reserved.

Published in the USA

ISBN: 9798633179330
Imprint: Independently published

Robertv1989@outlook.com

www.robertvillegas.com

Table of Contents

Introduction 4
Is Capitalism Moral? 9
- MASS PRODUCTION 12
- THE DIVISION OF LABOR 18
- THE LAW OF SUPPLY AND DEMAND 20
- CAPITAL ACCUMULATION 23
- THE FREE FLOW OF CAPITAL 26
- CORPORATE STRUCTURE 31
- MONETARY POLICY 33
- THE PRINCIPLE OF TRADE 41

Is Capitalism Evil? 47
- Laissez Faire Capitalism – Focus on Reality 47
- Mixed Economy - Skepticism/Progressivism 51
- Religious Conservatives – Focus on the Spiritual 61
- Summary of the Chapter 67

Beginning to Argue for Capitalism 71
- The Fallacy of Technocracy 75
- The Fallacy of Scarcity 78
- Life as Conflict 80
- The Fallacy of Social Justice 84
- The Appeal of Socialism Among the Young 86
- The Social Safety Net of Capitalism 89

Laissez nous Faire "Leave us Alone" 91
Capitalism, the Perfect System 98

Introduction

How many times have we heard the old saw: "Capitalism has failed again"? We heard it during the Great Depression of 1929 after Hoover's tariffs had precipitated economic retaliation and a banking crisis. Along with this question usually came a statement to the effect, that "We can fix capitalism and make it even stronger by issuing economic controls or spending money to stimulate economic activity."

We also heard this statement said by Barack Obama during the 2008 mortgage loan crisis. His solution was more economic intervention in the form of the Dodd-Frank Bill which imposed draconian regulations on the banking industry. Additionally, Obama's stimulus programs created one of the slowest and tepid of recoveries in the history of our nation.

The leftists who make these statements think they can get away with blaming capitalism for all of our ills. This book will argue that capitalism, as an economic system, cannot fail. In a fully free market, the rational actions taken by individuals, the very actions liberated by capitalism, cannot fail as long as the human mind seeks to ascertain reality and act upon its guidance. This book will also argue that the problems the leftists claim to be fixing are caused by the very interventionist programs they have introduced into the free dealings of men.

To begin, "...if an Englishman—or for that matter, any other man in any country of the world—says today to his friends that he is opposed to capitalism, there is a wonderful way to answer him: "You know that the population of this planet is now ten times greater than it was in the ages preceding capitalism; you know that all men today enjoy a higher standard of living than your ancestors did before the age of capitalism. But how do you know that you are the one out of ten who would have lived in the absence of capitalism? The mere fact that you are living today is proof that capitalism has succeeded, whether or not you consider your own life very valuable."[1]

The truth of this statement is important when one considers the efforts to destroy and replace capitalism by our politicians, college professors, intellectuals and street protestors. Because capitalism creates a surplus of products and money, people are able to survive while those living in non-capitalist countries die from starvation. This is because ideas have consequences especially for those who take moral lessons from them. If the idea creates peace and cooperation, then people are free to develop their lives by working together. If the idea is restrictive and coercive, then people have little incentive to produce because they are not allowed to keep the products of their work.

We have most likely all seen pictures of mobs carrying signs and banners, "Capitalism has Failed" and "Capitalism is Evil". Virtually none of the people carrying these signs would be alive today were it not for the fact that capitalism was allowed to flourish in the 19th

---

[1] Economic Policy Thoughts for Today and Tomorrow, Ludwig von Mises, Gateway Editions, Chicago Pages 5 - 6

century. None of us would have the benefit of modern medical science, automobiles, airplanes, cell phones, television, movies and the Internet were it not for the fact that the genesis of these life-saving modern instruments was an age of full unregulated capitalism. Capitalism is the moral idea.

Spending one's time denigrating capitalism, profits and production must be a horrible way to live, especially since one is trying to appeal to envy. Why would anyone hold as evil the very process of living and thriving? Why decide to live outside the system of plenty and declare oneself the moral authority that judges people as evil for living? What have you done in your life that you are complaining about people making money and enjoying their earnings? What is wrong with you?

What would happen if the world decided to do away with all profits? Do you know? The socialists, as leaders of society, would say that their system would still be able to generate all the wonderful products previously ascribed to capitalism. They would cry that their creation of "rights" to jobs, health care, education, day care, retirement, and whatever other "rights" they imagine, will create a new world of abundance for everyone. They assure us that they are kindly people who would never allow government to become dictatorial and oppressive like other socialist governments in the past. Their socialism would be "democratic"; kind and approved by the people. They would not dictate to or force anyone, and, this time, the people would vote on all measures.[2]

Today, young socialists eagerly declare themselves part of the "We Generation". They think that collective action will finally be accomplished because they, in their infinite wisdom, will finally make it work. They really mean it when they declare the victory of "the people" and they are going to make sure that the people get the socialism they want. Indeed, unlike the foolish people of the past, they really mean it *this time*; they intend to complete the promise of collective action through sacrifice. They declare their willingness to sacrifice for the "downtrodden" and they insist that the evil capitalist will finally be made to bear the yoke of sacrifice for "the people".

Needless to say, we foolish people of the past, chuckle at the naiveté of these promises and we note what we learned through experience. It is not difficult to point out that past socialist leaders also **meant** it. Indeed, they meant it so much they sent millions into the ovens, "showers", prisons and concentration camps – millions of people who were thought to be the enemies of socialism; the selfish people who did not chuckle as they were directed (by men with rifles) to get in line and experience the "justice" of the collective ideal known as socialism.

I wrote this book to provide the fundamental principles we will need during the coming years. These principles

---

[2] Ignoring the fact that most past systems promised the same thing.

are based, not on Marxist premises, but on the facts of how man survives and what these facts mean about building a proper society. I think it is important that hard working citizens learn the real issues that affect their lives and take definitive action to stop government when it steps out of bounds. The Constitution, as it was originally written, does not allow the government to violate the rights of citizens, even if those citizens are part of the "We Generation", wise, wonderful and self-sacrificial.

In this book, we are going to look at capitalism and decide if it is moral. We will look at it from the perspective of the individual and attempt to analyze the criticisms of capitalism made by those wise young socialists who seem to have all the answers. I will show that they know nothing about economics, history and how to build a moral system for man.

Is Capitalism Moral?

I hope you agree with me that proposals to make monumental changes in our economic system should be made while armed with verified facts. I ask my readers to clear the slate in their minds about the so-called evils of capitalism. As a young business executive, I decided to make sure I understood capitalism before I agreed to conduct business in our semi-capitalist economy. I suggest you do the same before you decide to throw a Molotov Cocktail through a bank window.

One of the negative things I heard about capitalism is that virtually all capitalists are like fly-by-night carnival barkers who cheat people in every town where they perform; safe in the knowledge that in a few days they will be in another town away from the people they cheated before. The idea is that capitalists are interested only in getting the buck and they don't care how they do it as long as they can lie and steal their way from deal to deal.

I learned early on that a capitalist business owner has an incentive to provide real value for his customers and he must be reliable, trustworthy and well-respected. In order to gain the trust of people, he must provide real value and hope that his product or service is good enough that he will gain a good reputation and lots of customer referrals. He cannot afford to be a fly-by-nighter because it is not good for business. I learned also that most capitalists are solid individuals who engage in honest dealings and, if they do make a mistake and disappoint a customer, they learn from their mistakes and do better the next time. I realized that capitalism was not about getting over on your customer, cheating him and then getting away. On the contrary, capitalism is a system that can only benefit the honest individual. I found that the Marxist view of capitalism as dog-eat-dog class warfare was a false view.

I also learned that there were several key aspects, or features, of capitalism that made it a moral economic system, and surprisingly, these features ensured that capitalism would lead to the creation of wealth only if the capitalist were an honest individual. In fact, each of those features required rational thought and reasoned action. In fact, they could only function so long as the capitalist was given free reign to think with his own mind; and this freedom was critical to the success of the capitalist. In other words, capitalism is moral because it requires moral behavior in production and trade relations.

"The capitalist system was termed "capitalism" not by a friend of the system, but by an individual who considered it to be the worst of all historical systems, the greatest evil that ever had befallen mankind. That man was Karl Marx. Nevertheless, there is no reason to reject Marx's term, because it describes clearly the source of the great social improvements brought about by capitalism. Those improvements are the result of capital accumulation; they are based on the fact that people, as a rule, do not consume everything they have produced, that they save—and invest—a part of it."³

The main business of American industry is production, not spending, not theft or forgery. Only the influence of an anti-capitalist philosophy that focuses moral worth upon sacrifice could cloud men's minds to the exacting kind of virtue required of people who choose to be productive. Only anti-capitalists who do not understand economic principles could declare that "Capitalism has failed again." Only haters of men could deny the fact that being productive is a virtue. In fact, production is a *high* virtue and it is beneficial to men who want a better life. Simply put, production is the creation of goods, products, services and values. None of those are evil and none of them "fail" when men are left free. Why, then, do Marxists and progressives think it is evil?

If you wonder why some CEOs make so much money under capitalism, it is because their leadership enables their corporations to successfully sell to and deliver quality products and services. Capitalism is about the efficient use of capital and that usage involves the efficient production of quality products, sold at prices that customers are willing to pay. If you think that just anyone can do this, you have no idea how to do it. Capitalism, the system based on human excellence, cannot fail. People may fail. Machines may fail, ideas may fail, but the economic and political system that liberates people to be self-sufficient, can never fail.

---

³ Economic Policy Thoughts for Today and Tomorrow by Ludwig von Mises, Gateway Editions, Page 10

Successful self-sufficiency can never fail. Freedom cannot fail.

It is the anti-man attitude of capitalism's detractors that moves many people to damn capitalism for being too concerned with materialistic things. Such detractors tell man he has produced too much and should give away the fruits of his production. It tells him that to produce is so easy, but to give so hard. Such a vapid argument is blind to man's true greatness because it refuses to regard production as an essential, necessary and highly desirable virtue. And because anti-capitalism does not protect the rights of people to be moral, it lets loose the most radical of Marxist haters; the people who would just as soon crush the skull of an honest man than ask him for a job.

It is this same anti-man philosophy that advocates a welfare-state to forcibly divest men of their incomes for the sake of the nonproductive. And, finally, it is the same philosophy that refuses to consider the truth that a capitalist society can do more good (even for the nonproductive) than any welfare society. To prove this last point, we will analyze some of the essential elements of capitalism, their causes, and their consequences. They are mass production, the division of labor, the law of supply and demand, capital accumulation, the free flow of capital, corporate organization, monetary policy and the principle of trade.

MASS PRODUCTION

Mass production is one aspect of capitalism for which socialists or fascists like to take credit. I mention this because they think the ability to mass produce is like a magic potion for socialist affluence. They promise that their "new" societies, based upon force, will produce abundance because their theft of capitalist machines and factories will enable them to produce products on a massive scale. All they have to do is install the confiscated machines in their stolen factories.

Yet, mass production is a uniquely capitalist invention that lowers the cost of production and spreads the benefits to virtually all parties in society. As a key factor of capitalist production, it requires capital, corporate structures, stable currency and the law of supply and demand, each of which socialism is incapable of creating. This is why we saw, during the early part of the last century, the failure of socialist economies. They could put machines into production but without the law of supply and demand, producers could not predict efficient pricing and production quotas. The result was insufficient capitalization, too much of some products and too little of others.

Mass production enables the "making" of complex products on an assembly line that employs well-trained workers, each performing a specific task in a pre-determined way. This efficiency results in the creation of automobiles, guns, farm machinery, turrets and lathes and even small products like cell phones, television sets and other electronic equipment sold cheaply. The benefit of the production process is that highly valued products can be made in a timely manner at a very low cost compared to products made by a single individual or small team.

Despite the fact that socialists declare capitalism to be about the rich making money at the expense of the poor, mass production is specifically aimed at the masses including the poor. It has also spawned such terms as mass marketing, global marketing and mass distribution so more products can be delivered to more people. What's more, mass production helps corporations make so much money, they can pay their employees more money which creates more customers for their products. Yet, mass production gives leftists the opportunity to declare that it is really the workers who are responsible for the riches of the capitalists. Although well trained workers are important to mass production, the key factor in the success of a corporation is leadership and the ability of leadership to correctly put capital resources to work, make them efficient and predict market forces.

When speaking about mass production in eighteenth century London, Mises avers:

"(Eighteenth century London) was the beginning of mass production, the fundamental principle of capitalistic industry. Whereas the old processing industries serving the rich people in the cities had existed almost exclusively for the demands of the upper classes, the new capitalist industries began to produce things that could be purchased by the general population. It was mass production to satisfy the needs of the masses."[4]

With the advent of mass production, the individual, for the first time in history, was able to purchase amazing products that benefited him tremendously. The anti-capitalist radicals who continuously proclaim a separation between rich and poor have completely missed the point that capitalism makes the lives of "the lower classes" better. Capitalism is truly the system that bridges the gap between rich and poor because it elevates the standard of living of every man and makes more products available to all men at prices most of them can afford.

The pioneers of mass production lines, businessmen like Henry Ford, Eli Whitney and many others, recognized that by lowering the costs of production through innovative processes, they could lower prices; which made their products available to the average man. On the other hand, the socialists missed the truth that mass production requires genius, not only in production, but also in marketing, packaging, logistics and other efficiencies that few individuals could accomplish. Automobiles, oil and gas products, household appliances, and in our time, computers and cell phones have made the lives of all people better and at very reasonable prices compared to the benefits. Mass production has made it possible for the average man today to live a life better than the kings and lords of the past.

---

[4] Economic Policy Thoughts for Today and Tomorrow, Ludwig von Mises, Gateway Editions, Chicago Page 3

A side benefit of mass production is that it makes products for other businessmen too. For instance, J.D. Rockefeller of Standard Oil, in his successful efforts to bring down the cost of producing kerosene, using a by-product of the refining process, created an opportunity for Henry Ford who needed an inexpensive fuel for his new Ford automobiles. Had not Rockefeller discovered the qualities of gasoline, a byproduct of the distilling process, and produced it in larger quantities for lower prices, Ford would never have been able to sell his cars at lower prices to the masses.

Ford's cars needed a cheap fuel and, before Standard Oil, other automobile fuels were too expensive for the average consumer. There was no private agreement between Rockefeller and Ford to do this; there was only the common principle of mass production that made it possible, releasing at the same time the energies of other men who could now improve their lives and be more productive. None of this could have been possible in a socialist system intent on preventing "evil" capitalists from making profits.

Yet, capitalism is constantly vilified for creating a gap between rich and poor while many people (previously poor) are now millionaires due to their innovative ideas and ingenuity. Capitalism is the only system that opened up the ability of every man to be productive. All they had to do was be willing to work. Capitalism even provided, free of charge to the workers, the new machines that created the new jobs for the poor. And if you were frugal in your spending, you could make money in a factory, save some of it and invest in other businesses that were growing. Eventually, you could take your money, start your own business and join the economic push for better products and services. You, the average man, could become rich.

To quote Ludwig von Mises:

"This is the fundamental principle of capitalism as it exists today in all of those countries in which there is a highly developed system of mass production: Big business, the target of the most fanatic attacks by the so-called leftists, produces almost exclusively to satisfy the wants of the masses. Enterprises producing luxury goods solely for the well-to-do can never attain the magnitude of big businesses. And today, it is the people who work in large factories who are the main consumers of the products made in those factories. This is the fundamental difference between the capitalistic principles of production and the feudalistic principles of the preceding ages."

Getting back to the idea that the communists and socialists thought they could nationalize the factories and successfully engage in mass production; the reason capitalism overtook communism is because capitalism improved the lives of more people than communism, made them happier, freer, more affluent and more productive. The communists, on the other hand, could not "bank" on mass production because they had neither a pricing mechanism nor efficient management due to cronyism and nepotism. They could not read the minds of the customers.

Communism, mired in the separation of classes, produced no such improvements in mass production. The workers, the people whom the violent communist revolutions were supposed to have given power, merely toiled in poorly maintained factories and dangerous working conditions. They refused to be productive for people who were skimming the fruits of their labor so they, the managers, could have better apartments, better vodka and better caviar for themselves.

When a government is at war with freedom, the first casualty of that war is the individual. The second casualty is mass production. Communism tried to steal the benefits of capitalism while promising to create a system that would beat it – but they forgot that the essential element of capitalism was freedom not the machines that they expropriated. And, since the masses were not free, not adequately paid, they were seldom able to purchase the inferior products of the collectivized workers. They were frustrated because the "managers" chose to produce products they did not demand. The socialized system was inefficient because it was not focused on production for the "masses" but instead was focused on mass production of unwanted inferior products. The result was long lines and cynicism.

THE DIVISION OF LABOR

At the base of any advanced civilization is the division of labor. The complexity that this division achieves, if it is based upon production, is an indication of that society's success. A tribe whose basic division is that of chief, witch doctor, hunters, and child raisers can hardly achieve the diversity necessary for a trip to the moon, although they often find good reason to worship the moon.

The advanced case of the division of labor must be distinguished from these crude forms found in primitive societies. The advanced forms represent more than an economic advance; instead an intellectual advance is required; an advance that is achieved by the men who realize that specific human resources can be much more efficiently employed if each individual devotes more time and study to specific delimited activities in cooperation with others who perform other delimited activities. It also requires the knowledge that, when the individual devotes his time and skills exclusively to one task, he will be able to create more valuable goods for trade with others including goods of knowledge.

As mentioned above, the advanced division of labor represents an intellectual achievement through which the best thinkers realize the potential benefit of an abstract idea and put it to use. The abstract idea becomes an established asset of the individual in society, a principle that makes it a better place in which to live, and if the division of labor is allowed to flourish without regulation, it adds increasing benefit to the life of every individual in that society. Multiply this by thousands of entrepreneurs engaged in millions of transactions and you have a thriving economy.

An individual specializing in a specific task can get more work done in a shorter period of time, can devote his time to improving his skills and timeliness and can, over time, improve the quality of his product and earn more money. This impacts the work done by others performing related tasks, making it possible for them to do more while benefiting from the work of the others. Cycles of excellence develop that grow exponentially over time.

THE LAW OF SUPPLY AND DEMAND

The Law of Supply and Demand is the fundamental process that is liberated by capitalism. This principle is made possible by a free market where each party has the option to choose his own actions and to interact and trade with other parties who are also freely participating. When people are free to make their own economic decisions, they can negotiate for the lowest price and purchase products they think will satisfy their needs. This sets up a process whereby the price of a product is set by the demands of consumers and by the number of such products available on the market. Briefly stated, if the supply of the product exceeds the demand for it, the price must fall until the customer wants to buy it. If the supply is lower than the demand for the product, the price must rise until it meets all the demands of consumers that can afford that price.

But there is more:

"When it comes to choosing between socialism and capitalism as an economic system, the problem is somewhat different. The authors of socialism never suspected that modern industry, and all the operations of modern business, are based on calculation. Engineers are by no means the only ones who make plans on the basis of calculations, businessmen also must do so. And businessmen's calculations are all based on the fact that, in the market economy, the money prices of goods inform not only the consumer, they also provide vital information to businessmen about the factors of production, the main function of the market being not merely to determine the cost of the last part of the process of production and transfer of goods to the hands of the consumer, but (also) the cost of those steps leading up to it. The whole market system is bound up with the fact that there is a mentally calculated division of labor between the various businessmen who vie with each other in bidding for the factors of production—the raw material, the machines, the instruments—and for the human factor of production; the wages paid to labor. This sort of calculation by the businessman cannot be accomplished in the absence of prices supplied by the market. (Parenthesis mine)

"At the very instant you abolish the market—which is what the socialists would like to do—you render useless all the computations and calculations of the engineers and technologists; the technologists can give you a great number of projects which, from the point of view of the natural sciences, are equally feasible, but it takes the market-based *calculations* of the businessman to make clear which of those products is the most advantageous, from the *economic* point of view."[5]

This "socialist" intervention into the market is accomplished by means of regulating the various factors of production within the modern industrial system. Whenever a government intervention takes place, it immediately starts a process of re-distribution which shifts economic power from the market and toward the supposed beneficiaries of the interventions. This destroys all market-based supply and demand calculations and begins a process of deterioration in the market that inevitably results in losses to all parties, with the cumulative impact of those interventions being the inability of businesspeople to plan their businesses, their production processes and their profits.

On the other hand, when the Law of Supply and Demand is allowed to function freely, the market sends signals to producers about the demand for their products and this helps them set prices and/or increase production to meet the demand. The Law of Supply and Demand can also signal to a producer that there is no demand for the product, in which case, the producer will go out of business, examine his marketing strategy to increase demand or reallocate his assets toward other productive purposes. These signals sent by the market create a free flow of products and enable consumers to have the products they need.

---

[5] Economic Policy – Thoughts for Today and Tomorrow by Ludwig von Mises, Gateway Editions, Softcover Pages 32-33

The nemesis of the Law of Supply and Demand is interference by government. Government can engage in price controls, other regulations and monetary inflation, all of which restrict the ability of the producer to receive the signals from the market that he needs to make good decisions.

CAPITAL ACCUMULATION

Capital accumulation works hand-in-hand with the division of labor, the law of supply and demand and mass production. The society that grasps this crucial economic principle and decides to allow capital accumulation - protected by property rights - is the most moral of societies. Of advanced economies, Mises tells us:

"...the difference (between capitalist and non-capitalist societies) is not personal inferiority or ignorance. The difference is the supply of capital, the quantity of capital goods available. In other words, the amount of capital invested per unit of the population is greater in the so-called advanced nations than in the developing nations."[6]

Through capital accumulation, men are able to invest their savings in ever more ambitious projects, and thereby produce hitherto unheard of goods and services. The entire society advances when those few who are able to accumulate vast amounts of wealth are

---

[6] Economic Policy – Thoughts for Today and Tomorrow by Ludwig von Mises, Softcover, Gateway Editions, Foreign Investment, Page 77

given the freedom to do so. In fact, capital accumulation is not restricted to the rich. Anyone can save his money and invest it. Indeed, it is the small investor, through his banks and savings institutions, who does most of the investing in a capitalist economy.

The principle of capital accumulation also exposes the lie that the rich get richer and the poor get poorer in a capitalist economy. In fact, everyone gets richer because there are always new job opportunities and new products to improve life and create enjoyment and relaxation. Contrast this to the statist society that is skimming surplus wealth through taxation and inflation of currency, wasting it and creating poverty in the process. Leftists routinely waste capital by spending it in re-distribution which sends money to people who do not save it but spend it on consumable products or drugs and alcohol.

Consider the low intellectual level of a government that holds profit to be exploitation, that only hard labor creates value and that the workers are exploited by the owners of capital resources. Any such society would be for expropriation and re-distribution to such a degree that capital accumulation would be destroyed – which means that society is destroyed. This was the low intellectual level of socialists and fascists of the last century. It is the low intellectual level of modern-day technocrats who think they have the ability to "manage" an economy.

"An often unrealized fact about capitalism is this: savings mean benefits for all those who are anxious to produce or to earn wages. When a man who accrued a certain amount of money—let us say, one thousand dollars—and, instead of spending it, entrusts these dollars to a savings bank or an insurance company, the money goes into the hands of an entrepreneur, a businessman, enabling him to go out and embark on a project which could not have been embarked on yesterday, because the required capital was unavailable."[7]

The result of the efficient use of capital is enhanced production, new products, increased wages and more capital savings. Needless to say, this is a process that can significantly improve employment and affluence. The workers attracted to new higher wages, become consumers of these new products and their lives are lifted as well. The entrepreneur, on the other hand, grows in his ability to organize profitable businesses and he must be supported by ever more efficient managers, partners and workers. When this process of using capital is restricted, let us say, by high taxation or monetary manipulation, the economy grows at a slower pace or declines.

Yet, it is not only the entrepreneur who must make efficient use of the capital lent to him by the savings bank. The savings bank must also make efficient use of the funds entrusted to it by making them available to borrowers with a record of successful use of money;

---

[7] Economic Policy Thoughts for Today and Tomorrow by Ludwig von Mises, Gateway Editions, Page 11

and, finally, the efficient use of capital also rests on the saver who must correctly choose the savings bank as a repository of his money. The idea that the rich get richer and the poor get poorer in capitalism, a basic Marxist tenet, is therefore false. *"A country becomes more prosperous in proportion to the rise in the invested capital per unit of its population."*[8]

THE FREE FLOW OF CAPITAL

Few people think that the free flow of capital is a civil or individual right. Few people fight for the right to do what they want with their capital. Few would die for that right or engage in civil disobedience over it or even protest for it. But, in truth, it is an important right for which men should fight. If we are to recover a proper society, we must demand it, fight for it and get out on the street for it.

The free flow of capital is the right of every individual to use his investment capital in any way he decides. It is such an important right that the capitalist system is thwarted without it. Capitalists hold that the government should protect it because it keeps people free and advances their abilities to live and prosper. It is essential to the growth and success of capitalists and workers, so much so that its frustration can destroy the capitalist system and the prosperity that comes with it.

Today, progressives and other leftists believe that government should restrict and control the flow of

---

[8] Ibid Page 14

capital to ensure that investment capital is used in a way that benefits the least among us. They hold that productive individuals should be forced to advance "social justice" over their own private profit. They ignore the truth that re-distribution of income destroys not only the free flow of capital, but, because of this, also destroys prosperity and it sends society into deeper and deeper poverty.

Why is this so? Let's try to understand how investment capital works in society. Who provides capital for investment? The answer is people who save their earnings so they can gain interest. These people include pension plans, individual savers from the middle class and upper classes and, finally, venture capitalists. This last group is usually called the 1% and despite the fact they are very small in number, they make the largest part of the income in society. For want of a better word, the 1% make up the people who work harder and smarter. They are inventive and hard-working people who have found the best way to use their money. They create the newest and best products, find the most efficient companies and invest their huge earnings in order to take advantage of those efficiencies and high profits. They are the real "worker bees" in society and they produce the bulk of the profits. Let's examine their impact on society.

Let's look at how the 1% earn their money.

The following chart shows how people earn their money.

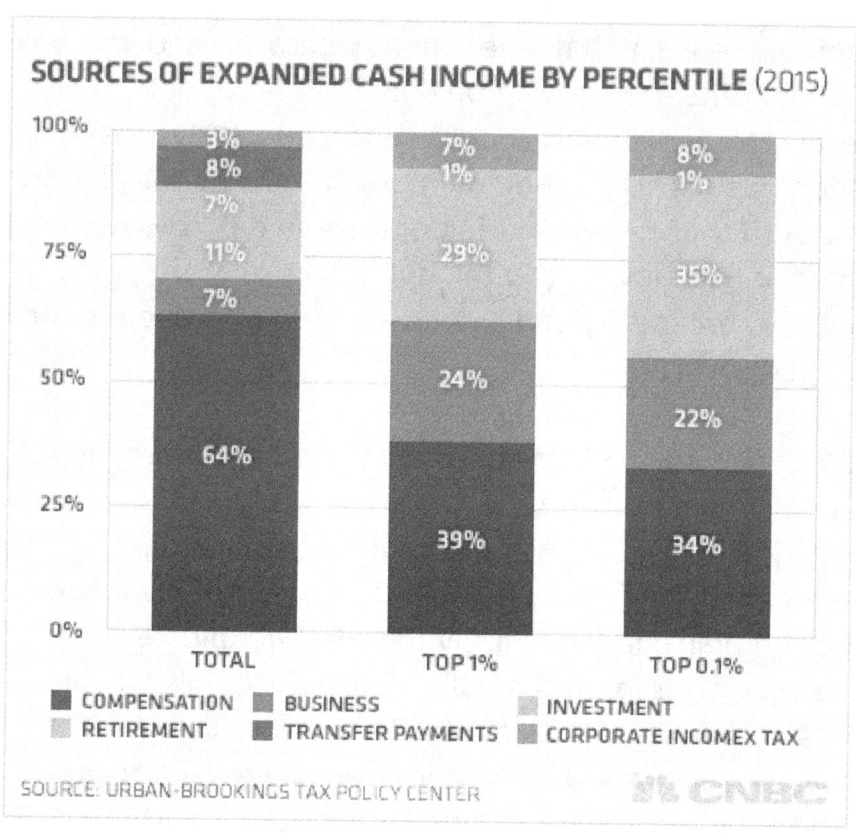

We see that the top 1% earn significantly more money from investments and from running their own businesses. On the other hand, the 99% earns more money from employment and they invest very little and even fewer of them run their own businesses. The implication of this is that the 1% invests better. They use their money smarter than the average employee and it reflects more earnings for them from capital investments.

The critical question is "why are we taking any money from the rich and giving it to the poor when most of the poor will spend their money in economically wasteful consumption?"

Remember the key difference between investment/production and consumption: The money invested in product creation is not consumed directly. It comes back to the investor along with profits. But the money spent on consumption does not come back to the spender; it is consumed – destroyed. This means that we lose the benefit of letting the 1% invest his or her money. That money is destroyed through consumption of the money he or she would normally invest.

Who pays the largest amount of taxes? As individuals, the top 1% pays the most taxes. But if we look at a percentage of the total taxes paid, here is what we get:

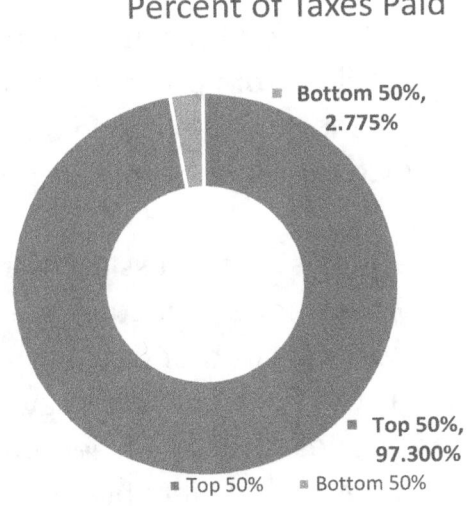

This data is taken from IRS data updated by FinancialSamuri.com on 1/27/15. It shows that the top 50% of people pay 97% of the taxes. This means that by punishing the very people who invest we are seriously affecting our economic stability and growth.

Government force through taxation and monetary inflation is a violation of the right to the free flow of capital. Additionally, it violates the freedom of expression, the freedom of association and property rights. Yet, the truth is that if you produce something and earn a profit, that profit should be yours to do with as *you* decide. The free flow of capital is the expression of your freedom to use your mind and survive to the best of your ability. The free flow of capital represents your right to use your property as you see fit.

In the macro sense, the free flow of capital means that money flows to its best uses when people are free to decide how best to live their lives. It represents the choice to remove capital from poor uses and put it to better uses. It is a choice for the individual to make and properly not a choice for the government to make.

The free flow of capital is an expression of individual choice of chosen values not a collective choice that decides upon the social goals that capital should serve. Every individual has the right to use his savings and surplus capital as he sees fit. These freedoms are individual rights that are as inalienable as are the rights to freedom of speech, freedom of association, belief and self-defense. In fact, all examples of self-defense and individual rights should include the right to the free flow of capital.

In 2020, when our government decided to create two trillion dollars and re-distribute it to the American workers, they took almost all of that money from capital investment. They violated the principle of the free flow of capital by deciding the uses for an amount of money so large that it would frustrate economic growth indefinitely into the future. It also established the principle of re-distribution for the sake of stimulus which violated the rights of investors to decide how to use their money. Power was given over to government technocrats who were made the "deciders" of all economic activity, who would be winners and who would be losers. They frustrated for an indefinite period the free flow of capital.

CORPORATE STRUCTURE

Corporate structure is the individualization of a group of people involved in a voluntary association. It involves a system of organization that maximizes productive output with efficiently maximized input. It organizes its resources into unique and efficient productive processes, staffed by well-trained and well-educated employees who are also well paid.

As with all corporate organizations, it begins with a Mission and a Vision that the leaders of the corporation use to define business units and structural organization. The logic of moving from Mission to business processes to the corporate Vision is the art of management. It is no small task.

Indeed, managing an efficient corporate structure requires a genius of its own. The corporation heads must discover and integrate the tools that will help in the achievement of the organization's Vision. The structure is, in effect, a mini-machine with each part performing a different function. If the heads are good engineers, they can keep the machine running smoothly while improving, altering, and adjusting it for more output over time. Some changes have to be made on the spot and require a special skill, the ability to integrate new knowledge as quickly as possible with the tried-and-true.

The corporation is the ultimate vehicle through which the division of labor and all other features of capitalism are brought to maximum effectiveness for the customer. Anyone who sees corporations as evil villains who practice racism, exploitation and shoddy deceptions does not understand the important and vital influence that economic freedom plays in the life of a corporation and even a nation. The political thugs and brutes who claim to represent the poor, the workers and the aged are actually killing the very institutions (corporations) that make our nation and economy stronger. These busy bodies who think they know what makes a society run are nothing more than destroyers. They have yet to learn that a society which defends individual rights is a capitalist society and that a capitalist society, by its nature, enables people to make their own decisions. A capitalist society does not require interference and is not predatory by nature. To give professional parasites power over our economic decisions is tantamount to doing the opposite of what society and individuals need.

Capitalism is the only system that can make effective use of the division of labor, the law of supply and demand, mass production, the use of capital, capital accumulation and corporate structure. No other economic or political system generates the efficient interaction between these essential principles of economic life the way capitalism does. In fact, these essentials function effectively *only* when individuals are allowed to make their own value choices and keep the fruit of their labor. You cannot legislate any of these principles into existence and force them upon a nation. Capitalism is the only system based upon freedom and moral living. It makes the principles of free trade possible.

MONETARY POLICY

Sound monetary policy is important to sustained growth in a controlled economy. However, controlled economies cannot ensure that leaders will follow sound policies over the long-term. To ensure that politicians cannot do damage to a society, the best policy is to restrict politicians from violating property and individual rights. When individual transactions are agreed upon by the individuals engaged in those transactions it ensures that no one is manipulating the value of money and goods. It also ensures that government does not engage in other dangerous policies such as re-distribution, taxation, political prosecutions and other interferences.

The practice of money manipulation by government is one of the major causes of failed economic policies. When interventionists play with the money supply, they wind up causing many of the problems which they blame on capitalism.

To illustrate the truth of this, we're going to look at history. Below is a summary of the events that took place in a country that tried to stimulate its economy by means of expanding the currency. I have edited some terms to remove the country and specific names:

"And, first, in the economic department. From the early reluctant and careful issues of paper we saw, as an immediate result, improvement and activity in business. Then arose the clamor for more paper money. At first, new issues were made with great difficulty; but, the dyke once broken, the current of irredeemable currency poured through; and, the breach thus enlarging, this currency was soon swollen beyond control. It was urged on by speculators for a rise in values; by demagogues who persuaded the mob that a nation, by its simple fiat, could stamp real value to any amount upon valueless objects. As a natural consequence a great debtor class grew rapidly, and this class gave its influence to depreciate more and more the currency in which its debts were to be paid.

"The government now began, and continued by spasms to grind out still more paper; commerce was at first stimulated by the difference in exchange; but this cause soon ceased to operate, and commerce, having been stimulated unhealthfully wasted away.

"Manufactures at first received a great impulse; but, ere

long, this overproduction and overstimulus proved as fatal to them as to commerce. From time to time there was a revival of hope caused by an apparent revival of business; but 'this revival of business was at last seen to be caused more and more by the desire of far-seeing and cunning men of affairs to exchange paper money for objects of permanent value. As to the people at large, the classes living on fixed incomes and small salaries felt the pressure first, as soon as the purchasing power of their fixed incomes was reduced. Soon the great class living on wages felt it even more sadly.

"Prices of the necessities of life increased: merchants were obliged to increase them, not only to cover depreciation of their merchandise, but also to cover their risk of loss from fluctuation; and, while the prices of products thus rose, wages, which had at first gone up, under the general stimulus, lagged behind. Under the universal doubt and discouragement, commerce and manufactures were checked or destroyed. As a consequence the demand for labor was diminished; laboring men were thrown out of employment, and, under the operation of the simplest law of supply and demand, the price of labor-the daily wages of the laboring class-went down until, at a time when price's of food, clothing and various articles of consumption were enormous, wages were nearly as low as at the time preceding the first issue of irredeemable currency.

"The (merchant) classes at first thought themselves exempt from the general misfortune. They were delighted at the apparent advance in the value of the goods upon their shelves. But they soon found that, as they increased prices to cover the inflation of currency and the risk from fluctuation and uncertainty, purchases became less in amount (in other words, people bought less of their products) and payments less sure; a feeling of insecurity spread throughout the country; enterprise was deadened and stagnation followed.

"New issues of paper were then clamored for as more, (drink is) demanded by a drunkard. New issues only increased the evil; capitalists were all the more reluctant to embark their money on such a sea of doubt. Workmen of all sorts were more and more thrown out of employment. Issue after issue of currency came; but no relief resulted save a momentary stimulus, which aggravated the disease. The most ingenious evasions of natural laws in finance which the most subtle theorists could contrive were tried-all in vain; the most brilliant substitutes for those laws were tried; "self-regulating" schemes, "interconverting" (mutual conversion into like denominations before a trade) schemes - all equally vain. All thoughtful men had lost confidence. All men were waiting; stagnation became worse and worse. At last came the collapse and then a return, by a fearful shock, to a state of things which presented something like certainty of remuneration to capital and labor. Then, and not till then, came the beginning of a new era of prosperity.

"Just as dependent on the law of cause and effect was the moral development. Out of the inflation of prices grew a speculating class; and, in the complete uncertainty as to the future, all business became a game of chance, and all business men, gamblers. In city centers came a quick growth of stock-jobbers (those who deal only with brokers or other jobbers) and speculators; and these set a debasing fashion in business which spread to the remotest parts of the country. Instead of satisfaction with legitimate profits, came a passion for inordinate gains. Then, too, as values became more and more uncertain, there was no longer any motive for care or economy, but every motive for immediate expenditure and present enjoyment. So came upon the nation the obliteration of thrift. In this mania for yielding to present enjoyment rather than providing for future comfort were the seeds of new growths of wretchedness: luxury, senseless and extravagant, set in: this, too, spread as a fashion. To feed it, there came cheatery in the nation at large and corruption among officials and persons holding trusts. While men set such fashions in private and official business, women set fashions of extravagance in dress and living that added to the incentives to corruption. Faith in moral considerations, or even in good impulses, yielded to general distrust. National honor was thought a fiction cherished only by hypocrites. Patriotism was eaten out by cynicism.

"Thus was the history of (country) logically developed in obedience to natural laws; such has, to a greater or less degree, always been the result of irredeemable paper, created according to the whim or interest of legislative assemblies rather than based upon standards of value permanent in their nature and agreed upon throughout the entire world. Such, we may fairly expect, will always be the result of them until the fiat of the Almighty shall evolve laws in the universe radically different from those which at present obtain.

"And, finally, as to the general development of the theory and practice which all this history records: my subject has been Fiat Money in (country); How it came; What it brought; and How it ended.

"It came by seeking a remedy for a comparatively small evil in an evil infinitely more dangerous. To cure a disease temporary in its character, a corrosive poison was administered, which ate out the vitals of (country's) prosperity.

"It progressed according to a law in social physics which we may call the "law of accelerating issue and depreciation." It was comparatively easy to refrain from the first issue; it was exceedingly difficult to refrain from the second; to refrain from the third and those following, was practically impossible.

"It brought, as we have seen, commerce and manufactures, the mercantile interest, the agricultural interest, to ruin. It brought on these the same destruction which would come to a Hollander opening the dykes of the sea to irrigate his garden in a dry summer.

"It ended in the complete financial, moral and political prostration of (country), a prostration from which only a (dictator) could raise it.

"But this history would be incomplete without a brief sequel, showing how that great genius profited by all his experience. When (the dictator) took the consulship the condition of fiscal affairs was appalling. The government was bankrupt; an immense debt was unpaid. The further collection of taxes seemed impossible; the assessments were in hopeless confusion. War was going on (several fronts). All the armies had long been unpaid, and the largest loan that could for the moment be effected was for a sum, hardly meeting the expenses of the government for a single day. At the first cabinet council (dictator) was asked what he intended to do. He replied, "I will pay cash (meaning gold and silver) or pay nothing." From this time he conducted all his operations on this basis. "He arranged the assessments, funded the debt, and made payments in cash; and from this time- during all the campaigns of (the war) there was but one suspension of specie payment, and this only for a few days. When the first great (deleted word) coalition was formed against the (country), (dictator) was hard pressed financially, and it was proposed to resort to paper money; but he wrote to his minister, 'While I live I will never resort to irredeemable paper.' He never did, and (country), under this determination commanded all the gold she needed. When (military defeat) came, with the invasion of the Allies, with war on her own soil, with a change of dynasty, and with heavy expenses for war and indemnities, (country), on a specie (gold and silver) basis, experienced no severe financial distress.

"If we glance at the financial history of France during the Franco-Prussian War and the Communist struggle, in which a far more serious pressure was brought upon French finances than our own recent Civil War put upon American finance, and yet with no national stagnation or distress, but with a steady progress in prosperity, we shall see still more clearly the advantage of meeting a financial crisis in an honest and straightforward way, and by methods sanctioned by the world's most costly experience, rather than by yielding to dreamers, theorists, phrase-mongers, declaimers, schemers, speculators or to that sort of "Reform" which is "the last refuge of a scoundrel.

"There is a lesson in all this which it behooves every thinking man to ponder."[9]

"But though there soon came a degree of prosperity-as compared with the distress during the paper-money orgy, convalescence was slow. The acute suffering from the wreck and ruin brought by (money inflation) in process of repudiation lasted nearly ten years, but the period of recovery lasted longer than the generation which followed. It required fully forty years to bring capital, industry, commerce and credit up to their condition when the Revolution began,..."[10]

If you agree that what happened in France before

---

[9] Fiat Money Inflation In France, Andrew Dickson White, Pamphleteers 1945 - A paper read before a meeting of Senators and Members of the House of Representatives of both political parties, at Washington, April 12, 1876 and revised and extended in 1914.
[10] Ibid

Napoleon can happen here, please let people know about the booklet "Fiat Money Inflation in France". We need "thinking men" who can recognize the folly of today's policies and stop them.[11]

Also note that the rich, the very people that France needed to invest in the future, left the country during this period of inflation in France. Likewise, our leaders, in inflating the currency, are not making things better. Their actions are known by competent economists around the world to be the very actions that make things worse; we are talking here of massive unemployment, decline of our standard of living, food lines, starvation, rampant crime and corruption in our future.

You are being lied to, you are being bamboozled; you are being made into the fool of history if you do not protest the ignorant and destructive economic policies of the Federal government.

THE PRINCIPLE OF TRADE

Sometime during a primordial period, men learned the principle of trade. This principle holds that men seek value in trade with others. It was learned that if men are to live in society together, they must adhere to the idea that cooperation is the key to successful interactions and that all barter arrangements are consensual.

---

[11] http://amzn.to/23tBUeX

Say's Law is simply this: "A product is no sooner created, than it, from that instant, affords a market for other products to the full extent of its own value."[12] In other words, production leads to demand; and in particular, not the other way around.

In another formulation of the same law, Say wrote:

"As each of us can only purchase the productions of others with his own productions – as the value we can buy is equal to the value we can produce, the more men can produce, the more they will purchase."[13]

The reason this law is so central to capitalist ideology is because it counters and refutes the idea that consumption leads to demand which is the basic premise of re-distribution and cronyism, the idea that social goals take precedence over individual self-determination.

First, we must understand that advocates of central planning, socialism and all forms of statism need to reverse the commonly known causal relationship between production and demand in order to justify their thefts and re-distribution. They must educate people to believe that re-distribution spurs economic growth because the money is given to people who will spend it.

Yet, the left's claim that demand spurs supply cannot possibly be true. Even if it were accepted by the bulk of

---

[12] *A Treatise on Political Economy* (*Traité d'économie politique*) Page 138
[13] Ibid Page 3

humanity that production comes first, all counterarguments would support the concept of individual rights and that government has no authority to appropriate any man's money for any purpose whatsoever. Say's Law says, essentially that there are negative consequences from a violation of man's individual (property) rights.

In truth, production must come before consumption and any effort to spur production by means of spurring consumption fails because putting consumption first requires the expropriation of money from the productive (which restricts production). The effort to spur economic activity through re-distribution fails because it represents a mere transfer of money from one party to another. Both parties would have spent that money in some way and there is generally a net loss because the money is taken from productive people who would likely spend it more intelligently than those to whom it is given.

Capitalism is the only system that can make effective use of the division of labor, the law of supply and demand, mass production, the use of capital, capital accumulation and corporate structure. No other economic or political system generates the efficient interaction between these essentials of economic life the way capitalism does. In fact, these essentials function effectively *only* when individuals can make their own value choices and keep the fruit of their labor. You cannot legislate any of these principles into existence and force them upon a nation. Capitalism is the only system based upon freedom and moral living.

The principle of trade holds that men succeed at survival when their work activity improves their lives or makes them capable of more production. They trade with other men with the same motivation to survive and this spurs intelligent production and economic activity compared to a person who does not produce at a high level. These people, the less productive, often spend their gift of money on consumables which destroys the value of the money because the consumables are destroyed. That same money invested by its producer would have gone back to the investor with a profit.

The principle of trade means that products are exchanged by mutual consent. People are free to buy and sell with the expectation that trades are mutually agreed upon. In the vast majority of cases, both parties obtain a desired value. The result of millions of these mutual trades is a general improvement of the lives of individuals. The principle of trade implies that the individual is free to decide upon his or her self-interest with the assurance that, if he is intelligent about his choices, his life will constantly improve.

The idea that trade implies harm to someone neglects the basic principle of human interaction, the principle that makes economic coexistence possible; the principle of free trade for mutual benefit. When people engage in trade, they each expect to gain from the transaction. The standard of living in those countries that have free trade policies is evidence that mutual benefit does take place and that the capitalist world is not a den of thieves.

In fact, modern technocrats are limited and primed for failure by their medieval view of moral action. Their adherence to a "zero-sum" view of economic transactions means they are biased against trade of any kind. This turns trade into a hostile act beset with conflict and exploitation. But it also ignores the truth that most transactions involve money which means that both parties choose the values they will acquire in the transaction, so if they exchange money, they can still buy values; they can still act rationally and the zero-sum view falls apart.

With money as the medium for transactions, the choice about what to buy with the money earned can be delayed until the individual has made a careful evaluation of what he needs. So money enables better transactions with better outcomes. The only question is whether the amount of money involved in any transaction is adequate for that particular transaction. To help in this we have the law of supply and demand. The customer can consider his cost of production and measure that against what he or she is willing to pay for the product. To help, he has the testimony of other buyers and, based upon this, he can determine a price he considers fair. His fellow-trader has similar considerations on his side of the sale and both traders come to a workable price.

There is no reason to believe that man is flawed, that he cannot make the right decisions and that trade is a zero-sum proposition. Capitalism is not a zero-sum game; it is a system of trade wherein men constantly advance their ability to survive and solve the problems of survival. It is only when government slowly cuts away mutual trade to mutual benefit through regulation and taxation that society devolves into imperfection and incompetence. It is both the progressive and conservative views that make man into an enemy and seek to exploit his production for the sake of charlatans and criminals.

Is Capitalism Evil?

The type of economic system you advocate is determined by your view of man's nature and what it makes possible in terms of the economic actions of men in society. The ultimate question should be whether it enables effective moral action which leads to survival. Essentially, there are three positions: Laissez Faire Capitalism, Mixed Economy and Religious Conservatives.

Laissez Faire Capitalism – Focus on Reality

When I write of Laissez Faire Capitalism, I refer to more than just an economic viewpoint. I am referring to a philosophy about the nature of man and what that nature means for his survival. I am also not writing about today's conservatives but, more closely, about the kind of liberals who existed before the left (FDR and others) tried to appropriate the term liberals for themselves. I'm talking about the original free market advocates. They were called Classical Liberals.

Classical liberals were the original conservatives but they consisted of a group of intellectuals who fostered, not religion, but laissez faire capitalism. These men consisted of Adam Smith, Robert Turgot, Jean Baptiste Say, Freidrich Hayak, Ludwig von Mises, Henry Hazlitt and Ayn Rand to name a few.

In a sense, classical liberals were moralists. By defining the principles of trade among individuals and productive institutions (companies), they found the key elements which made possible the principles of human interaction and human striving in society. They realized that if men were given economic freedom, widely known as individual rights, they could solve their own problems more efficiently; and, most importantly, if they could trade with each other freely, they could offer ever-improving products to lift man out of squalor and poverty. Adam Smith began the quest for moral living in society by defining the principles of trade that made up proper living.

An economist identifies the principle of cause and effect as it relates to how and why men decide to produce things to trade with others. The economist's job is to show you the consequences of both free action and government action and to contrast the two. Additionally, within the realm of free trade, the economist can teach the producer how to maximize his effort, how to use the principles of free trade, as I discussed in my chapter above, most efficiently. The study of economics is a worthwhile activity that can improve the lives of countless people seeking to maximize their economic liberties.

One of the premier economists in history was Ludwig von Mises whose seminal work, *Human Action*[14], analyzed economic action in society and showed that capitalism was the superior system. His other works, including "Socialism"[15], "Bureaucracy"[16] and "Planning

---

[14] https://amzn.to/2X5EA9P
[15] https://amzn.to/3bPFHig
[16] https://amzn.to/2R81BoY

for Freedom[17]" are invaluable in helping you understand capitalism and its unmatched benefits; but they also describe how and why government intervention into the economy can cause harm to human flourishing.

Yet, Mises has one major flaw. He bases his economic ideas on a philosophy he calls praexeology which has a strong Kantian base. Praexeology is a euphemism for pragmatism (or human action). It holds that man makes economic decisions through trial and error and not by means of reason and rational decisions. Mises would hold that these (trial and error) decisions would, over time, result in the best outcomes but his de-emphasis on reason leaves much to be desired. He literally dismisses reason as a fundamental factor in decision-making.

To learn about the value of reason in society, we need to read Ayn Rand's Capitalism: the Unknown Ideal[18]. Rand would tell you:

"I am not primarily an advocate of capitalism, but of egoism; I am not primarily an advocate of egoism, but of reason. If one recognizes the supremacy of reason and applies it consistently, all the rest follows."

In fact, Ayn Rand was one of the key influences on the Tea Party of the last decade and, although she was not the dominant influence in that group, she did have many advocates that I call New Capitalist Radicals who hold a principled approach to individual rights and the

---

[17] https://amzn.to/2JDwgq0
[18] https://amzn.to/3bNzzH5

relationship between reason and human action. She opposed the view that man has a "tragic flaw" like some conservatives.

Laissez Faire Capitalism countenances no regulations. Rand's capitalists would tell you man must have capitalism because he has the capability of reason while conservatives tell you that he must have capitalism because he is susceptible to making mistakes. The capitalist argument stands for reason and its role in human living while the conservatives say that capitalism is right because man can be wrong.

"Yet, the question regarding man's nature is the foundation upon which all human action must be based. The answer to that question indicates not only how intellectuals think men will act but how governments will treat them. Does man have rights? Is he to be a slave to the needs of others? These questions are important. The only difference between conservatives and progressives is not that progressives see certain institutions as needing change and that conservatives do not; the vital question is "from where does man derive his mandate for moral action?" Political debates and revolutionary change are not about merely changing institutions; they are about understanding man's nature and dealing with him accordingly.

"When (a progressive) says he believes in service to the community, working for and dying for others, the conservatives can only say, 'so do we'. They may counter the progressives with arguments for faith, hope and charity, but the progressives also talk about faith, hope and charity. (Parenthesis mine)[19]

With this view of man, laissez faire society relies on the principles of capitalism that we advanced in the chapter "Is Capitalism Moral". Freedom is an unalienable right. This means that it is right for man to be free and this realization is based upon an immutable fact that no society or government can change. As Rand tells us, you can't force a mind. In order for man to use his mind to accomplish survival, he must be free to take the actions his mind deems appropriate to the achievement of his values, the highest value of which is life.

Mixed Economy - Skepticism/Progressivism

Today, the liberals advocate a coercive state that combines government intervention and free markets. This system creates a "slow creep" towards more and more coercive measures that use the economic system to "buy votes" at the expense of those who produce in the economy.

In the past, leftist intellectuals and politicians "stole" the term "liberal" from the conservatives. In my book, The Conservative's Dilemma, I wrote about this appropriation:

"In her excellent book (The Forgotten Man) on the Great Depression, historian Amity Shlaes discusses an

---

[19] The Conservative's Dilemma by Robert Villegas https://amzn.to/2R9i9gp

important theme that resounded throughout the difficult years of the Great Depression. She reprises a theme put forward by philosopher William Graham Sumner about the forgotten man of the era. She writes:

""About half a century before the Depression, a Yale philosopher named William Graham Sumner penned a lecture against the progressives of his own day and in defense of classical liberalism (the group we discussed above). The lecture eventually became an essay, titled "The Forgotten Man." Applying his own elegant algebra of politics, Sumner warned that well-intentioned social progressives often coerced unwitting average citizens into funding dubious social projects. (Parenthesis mine)

"Sumner wrote:

"'As soon as A observes something which seems to him to be wrong, from which X is suffering, A talks it over with B, and A and B then propose to get a law passed to remedy the evil and help X. Their law always proposes to determine...what A, B, and C shall do for X." But what about C? There was nothing wrong with A and B helping X. What was wrong was the law, and the indenturing of C to the cause. C was the forgotten man, the man who paid, "the man who never is thought of.

""In 1932, a member of Roosevelt's brain trust, Ray Moley, recalled the phrase, although not its provenance. He inserted it into the candidate's first great speech. If elected, Roosevelt promised, he would act in the name of "the forgotten man at the bottom of the economic pyramid." Whereas C had been Sumner's forgotten man, the New Deal made X the forgotten man-the poor man, the old man, labor or any other recipient of government help."[20]

"Many think that this focus on the consumer rather than the producer is the very idea that prolonged the depression. I submit that this shift away from the real forgotten man, the enlightened producer, is the very essence of progressivism. As a result of this shift our nation has been poorly served by politicians. In fact, there is a forgotten "ism" that parallels the forgotten man. Where the forgotten man for the progressives was the slave, the hard working American, who silently fed the nation, the forgotten "ism" was the philosophical fountainhead that had to be silenced so that conservatives and progressives could accomplish their baseless enslavement of the individual. These ideas, reason, the efficacy of the senses, individualism, natural rights and limited government, born in the Enlightenment, had successfully liberated the mind and the body of man so he could flourish and prosper. With progressives and especially with the New Deal, these ideas had to be removed from consideration. That forgotten "ism" is "liberalism", the original philosophy that fostered limited government, liberty and capitalism."[21]

In my book, What Harvard and Princeton Don't Want you to Know, I wrote about empiricists and skeptics:

---

[20] The Forgotten Man, Amity Shlaes, Harper Perennial, paperback Page 12
[21] Ibid Page 11

"...(Empiricism) derives from what I call secular forms of religion. It concludes that *ideas* have no consequence in the real world and, as with religion, men should recognize that it is not possible for the individual to attain knowledge and values that are relevant to life. Empiricism is a result of the dichotomy in religion between the spiritual and the real.... ...Religious thinkers thought that ideas from the spiritual realm were purer and more important than ideas that related to this world which were considered inferior, impure and evil. The empiricist merely chooses to accept the real world as it is but holds that we cannot learn anything about it. (Parenthesis mine)

"David Hume (1711-1776) is considered to have been a hard-nosed empiricist who strictly adhered to facts. I submit that Hume's empiricism elevated context dropping into common practice and led the world into a dead end with devastating consequences. After Hume, there were few who argued that his method was wrong, that his logic was skewed and few men even realized the real damage to real people that was to come. Religion preached a dictatorship of God, Hume, through his followers preached an actual dictatorship of monstrous murderers. Either way, it was a dictatorship.

"Hume began his philosophical quest by attempting to examine the issues that relate to how man can develop certainty. Though most philosophers assume that Hume was led to his conclusions through rigorous empirical analysis, the truth is that Hume starts with the premise that there is something wrong with human thinking and then he builds his philosophy around that preconceived notion to conclude that there is something wrong with human thinking. He posits that man's ignorance is created by the inefficacy of human memory. He says sensations are immediate, felt strongly, felt as real, but our recollection of them, our thinking, is fuzzy and this must be why people disagree; why they are contradictory and ignorant in the use of their minds. What he accomplished was to give skeptics the "certainty" needed to blatantly state that there was no certainty. The average man was left blind and incapable of thinking. And since man was incapable of reason, they thought, why should we even teach people how to think? We should merely demand their obedience.

"Hume revealed his view that we are basically fallible when he noted that his study was intended to provide a way for man to gain certainty but then concluded that there was only a fuzzy connection between ideas and impressions. He laid the foundation for an approach to induction that did nothing to advance induction or the acquisition of knowledge. Where scientists during his time, were practicing scientific induction, were discovering whole areas of new knowledge and reaching new heights of understanding, Hume was saying that we could only look at concrete facts. While businessmen had the vision and intelligence to take inductively derived knowledge and create whole new industries and magnificent new inventions, Hume was teaching us that there is no necessity, no connection between cause and effect, because we can't see it.

"This conclusion came to him while he sought to develop an impenetrable science that would rid the world of superstition. Yet, he provided us with a new form of doubt as the foundation of science and inquiry. Consider David Hume's views about necessity and the "inability" of man to understand reality. Hume held that there are no valid inferences in the jump from observed cases to unobserved cases, from observed specifics to generalization. Building upon his premise that impressions are superior to ideas, Hume used what he thought was "pure" empirical observation as a source of knowledge while denigrating the value of induction and conceptually developed knowledge. So, according to Hume, science becomes arbitrary expressions of arbitrarily derived generalizations.

"For Hume, because we could not see necessity, there is no necessity, there is no source of human knowledge; there *is* no human knowledge. The hard-headed empiricist joins with the faithful rationalist. Hume:

> ""We must submit to this fatigue in order to live at ease ever after: And must cultivate true metaphysics with some care in order to destroy the false and adulterate….Accurate and just reasoning is the only catholic remedy, fitted for all persons and all dispositions; and is alone able to subvert that abstruse philosophy and metaphysical jargon, which, being mixed up with popular superstition, renders it in a manner impenetrable to careless reasoners, and gives it the air of science and wisdom.

> ""It is remarkable concerning the operations of the mind that, though most intimately preset to us, yet, whenever they become the object of reflection, they seem involved in obscurity; nor can the eye readily find those lines and boundaries, which discriminate and distinguish them. The objects are too fine to remain long in the same aspect or situation; and must be apprehended in an instant, by a superior penetration, derived from nature, and improved by habit and reflexion. It becomes, therefore, no inconsiderable part of science barely to know the different operations of the mind, to separate them from each other, to class them under their proper heads, and to correct all that seeming disorder, in which they are involved....And if we can go no farther than this mental geography, or delineation of the distinct parts and powers of the mind, it is at least a satisfaction to go so far; and the more obvious this science may appear (and it is by no means obvious) the more contemptible still must the ignorance of it be esteemed, in all pretenders to learning and philosophy..."

"What did Hume discover that provided man with a scientific base?

> ""Every one will readily allow, that there is a considerable difference between the perceptions of the mind, when a man feels the pain of excessive heat, or the pleasure of moderate warmth, and often he afterwards recalls to his

memory this sensation, or anticipates it by his imagination.

""These faculties may mimic or copy the perceptions of the sense, but they never can entirely reach the force and vivacity of the original sentiment...The most lively thought is still inferior to the dullest sensations."[22]

"So, where rationalism ends with blind emotion, Empiricism begins with it.

"Hume's method of deception is difficult to detect, but it consists of establishing a false context for human understanding by positing two non-essential concepts as if they were opposites. The attack starts at the outset of his book A Treatise of Human Nature. In Part 1, Of Ideas, their Origin, Composition, Connexion, Abstractions, &, Section 1, Of the Origin of our Ideas, Hume writes:

""All the perceptions of the human mind resolve themselves into two distinct kinds, which I shall call IMPRESSIONS and IDEAS. The difference betwixt these consists in the degrees of force and liveliness, with which they strike upon the mind, and make their way into our thought or consciousness. Those perceptions, which enter with most force and violence, we may name impressions; and under this name I comprehend all our sensations, passions and emotions, as they make their first appearance in the soul. By *ideas* I

---
[22] David Hume, An Inquiry Concerning Human Understanding, edited by I. A. Selby-Bigge (Clarendon Press, Oxford, 1894)

mean the faint images of these in thinking and reasoning; such as, for instance, are all the perceptions excited by the present discourse, excepting the immediate pleasure or uneasiness it may occasion. I believe it will not be very necessary to employ many words in explaining this distinction."

The empiricists' view of man as deficient in his ability to ascertain reality caused them to retain the views of man sponsored by the Church and led them to the concept of duty as the prime moral injunction. Men, in doing their duty, were charged with the responsibility of willingly sacrificing their lives for the next phase of the Hegelian/Marxist historical process. They were required to give their lives to the destruction of capitalism and the elevation of a society dependent upon the concept of human sacrifice.

The influence of the Church on the empiricists is seldom discussed in philosophical works about Hume and Kant but it is clear that many empiricists were religious and they had no problem countenancing the view of the imperfectability of man and the need for the state to make man do right.

On the other hand, the pragmatists among the skeptics picked up this same view of man to advocate a distorted view of the practical. For pragmatists, man could only do right by advancing an open society on the issue of developing knowledge. Since man could not see the connection between cause and effect, they thought, the only thing he could do is take blind leaps in action, and since man was a part of the collective, "the greatest good of the greatest number" became the clarion call for altruism, collectivism and a centrally planned society advancing the collective good.

Since it was society (the collective of minds) that determined reality for pragmatists, whatever it decided was sacrosanct and the end that society promoted required indoctrination and "group think". A good leader, under this scheme, was proficient at calculating the will of the people and forcing the unwilling to obey. The end justified the means and anything that advanced that end was deemed to be "good" or "moral". Duty became the clarion call for all men. This is the progressive/skeptic/pragmatist view of man. The only way to advance civilization, under this view, is to have a government that uses force to "centrally plan" society and economics.

Yet, the most culpable villains in the socialist scheme, today, are the CEOs of the Business Roundtable who have declared a new definition of capitalism. For these pragmatists, eager to be liked for their "realism", the only truth is social truth and the only justice is social justice; which signals their eager willingness to put their necks on the chopping block which is capitulation to altruism and collectivism. These men, who declare themselves to be representatives of our free economy are not capitalists. They are sellouts.

Religious Conservatives – Focus on the Spiritual

The flaw for the conservatives is simply the fact that their "tragic flaw" argument (which countenances some regulations) just as easily fosters socialism. I wrote about conservative Thomas Sowell's position in my book, The Conservatives Dilemma. I start with a quote from Dr. Sowell about progressive intellectuals:

""[Their] vision of society, in which there are many "problems" to be "solved" by applying the ideas of morally anointed intellectual elites is by no means the only vision, however much that vision may be prevalent among today's intellectuals. A conflicting vision has co-existed for centuries—a vision in which the inherent flaws of human beings are the fundamental problem and social contrivances are simply imperfect means of trying to cope with that problem—these imperfections themselves being products of the inherent shortcomings of human beings."[23] (Brackets mine)

"Professor Sowell takes for himself the position of the conflicting vision. His preferred vision of man is "...the tragic vision of the human condition that is very different from the vision of the anointed."[24] And, indeed, he joins a long tradition of philosophers and intellectuals who have shared that vision of human beings as inherently flawed. Unfortunately, a fact that

---

[23] Intellectuals and Society, Thomas Sowell, Basic Books, hardcover page 77
[24] Ibid Page 77

he seems to have missed is that this tragic vision of man is also held by the progressives.

"I wonder what he would say if I pointed out that the exalted view that intellectuals hold of themselves is not the same view they have of man. Their view of man derives from philosophers such as Kant, Hume and Marx that see men as intellectually incompetent, bereft of the ability to understand reality or the victims of economic factors outside of their control. None of those could be considered an exalted view of man.

(In fact, if you ask some of these conservatives to define their view of man, they will openly quote Hume's view as their inspiration for their advocacy of capitalism, i.e. Dinesh De Souza.) (Parenthesis mine)

"You have to ask yourself what is the point of taking the position that man is inherently flawed? Why would conservatives want to start with this premise? And more importantly, why do they think that this position provides a better argument for limited government and capitalism (when it is the same position that argues for statism)? (Parenthesis mine)

"As a former Catholic, I am familiar with this view. According to the Church, man is a sinner who would wreak havoc if left to his own "selfish" devices. His only moral constraint is that given to him by God and the church. According to this view, man must follow the Ten Commandments handed down to him by God through Moses. If men do not follow God's Commandments, God will punish them on this earth and after death. Men will only do right because of fear of God's wrath.

"Sowell asserts that the vision of contemporary intellectuals (progressives) today is based on an ages old view that sees problems as an outgrowth of social institutions. "In this vision, oppression, poverty, injustice and war are all products of existing institutions—problems whose solutions require changing those institutions, which in turn require changing the ideas behind those institutions."[25] Is Professor Sowell saying that the progressive view is one of hope and that their recommendations are part of some sort of exalted view about actually solving problems? Are we to assume that progressive criticism of institutions such as capitalism and the church are valid? Is he perhaps giving them too much credit? Claiming to have hope for man by forcing him to sacrifice, as the progressives do, is hardly a hopeful concept. Such a hope sounds like a politician's false promise never to come true.

"One must wonder if progressives today really threaten to destroy the most advanced, the most just and affluent civilization in the history of the world out of hope for a better future. There is a problem with cause and effect here.

"Whether you receive your view of man's nature from Hobbes or Hume, you cannot derive the principles of a free society and the anti-principles of a slave society from the same source; from the view that man is imperfect. The logic of ideas in practice is inexorable;

---

[25] Ibid Page 76

you cannot get around it. If the conservatives and the progressives both have the same basic view of man, the result will be the same social solution...and it is not hope but rubble.

"The dilemma for the conservatives on this issue is that they've failed to identify the principles that truly reflect what is wrong with the progressive views. They are on the same side as the progressives because they both advocate altruism as their fundamental principle. They have failed to recognize that man's true nature is not that he is imperfect but that he is a creature of reason, a creature perfectly suited for survival and success. The result: the conservatives have nothing to offer against the views of the progressives who also see man as cognitively incapable of understanding reality.

"To continue with Doctor Sowell, "In the tragic vision, barbarism is always waiting in the wings and civilization is simply "a thin crust over a volcano." "(This quote is from Havelock Ellis. The full statement is "All civilization has from time to time become a thin crust over a volcano of revolution.") The metaphor, "a thin crust over a volcano" used to describe the position of civilization against barbarism is illustrious of the problem that conservatives create for themselves. If civilization is truly a thin crust over a volcano, then what is the point of trying to create a better society? Eventually, the volcano will erupt (into revolution) and destroy that thin layer. If this is our choice, then why should we continue living on that thin crust? (parentheses mine)

"Unfortunately, this is the false alternative that conservatives create for themselves. A "thin crust" versus an inevitable explosion is hardly a choice. When they create such false alternatives based on non-essentials, they end up rationalizing false views and eventually taking the side of the progressives. To place one's enemies, the enemies of freedom, in the position of "a volcano", means you know they will win.

"Is civilization truly "a thin crust over a volcano"? Or are the principles of a proper society based upon something more fundamental in man's nature that must be recognized and accommodated by government; facts and principles that endure and never explode. Shouldn't we instead strive for a vision of man that will acknowledge his value and thereby help in the creation of a bulwark against the explosion of violence and barbarism? I submit that this bulwark is what the Founders of our nation attempted to create and their vision of man was not at all "tragic".

""In the tragic vision, social contrivances seek to restrict behavior that leads to unhappiness, even though these restrictions themselves cause a certain amount of unhappiness. It is a vision of trade-offs, rather than solutions, and a vision of wisdom distilled from the experiences of the many rather than the brilliance of a few."[26]

This means that civilization is nothing more than "social contrivances" designed to restrict immoral living in order

---

[26] Ibid Page 78

to make a trade-off, to create a balance between immorality (selfishness) and self-sacrifice (the good). What is being traded here is your decision to be productive in return for the government getting a piece of your production. Your punishment for committing the crime of surviving is that you have to pay people who cannot survive. Remember, this is the conservative view. And, to prove it, notice that the desire of (the progressives) to "re-distribute" wealth is considered by the conservatives to be "the brilliance of a few"." (Parenthesis mine)

Paul describes man's dilemma without knowing it: "For now we see through a glass, darkly, but then face to face: now I know in part; but then shall I know even as also I am known. And now abideth faith, hope, charity, these three; but the greatest of these is charity."[27]

Here you have it; man sees as through a glass darkly and is left only with faith, hope, charity – not with capitalism or freedom or even self-sufficiency. The three principles of the conservatives are the same as the three principles of the progressives. This is why these two sides are unable to defeat one another; they are on the same side; the side of self-sacrifice, not freedom or the pursuit of happiness; not self-sufficiency and independence but sacrifice of body and mind to the collective.

This contradiction of conservativism, that man has a tragic flaw, is the main point of separation between conservatives on one hand and the "laissez faire

---

[27] 1 Corinthians 13.12, 13

capitalists" on the other. Laissez faire capitalism holds that man has the ability to make reasoned decisions, he can think and decide what is in his self-interest. The conservative view is opposed to the idea of man as a creature of reason because, without God, men would choose their actions according to their self-interest. Both progressives and conservatives know that there is no reason *in reason* for men to sacrifice.

"The defenders of capitalism do not know that a rational, moral code of ethics is possible. They are, for the most part, altruists themselves. They adhere to the ideas of altruistic self-sacrifice--so much so that it blinds them to the true nature of capitalism and forces them into the position of being condescending but cheery opponents of men who are neither condescending nor cheery in their hatred of freedom and capitalism.

Summary of the Chapter

"Altruism is not the moral base of a capitalist system. We can't have a successful capitalist system if we just want to help people. Capitalism requires an independent mind. We must want men to be free to think, we must know living requires work, we must honor the independent mind and we must give credit where credit is due. Altruism requires a mind ruled by the edicts of superiors and it tells man that to be moral he only needs to follow the easiest path of all: the road of sacrifice as virtue. Capitalism requires integrity. Altruism requires that man fight his bodily nature with his spiritual code. Capitalism requires honesty. Altruism requires that one deceive one's own mind. Capitalism requires justice. Altruism requires that justice be suspended among men, that men do society's work by being unjust towards those who refuse to sacrifice. Capitalism requires productiveness. Altruism requires that the productive give away their money. Capitalism requires pride. Altruism requires both humility in some men and pretentiousness in others. Capitalism requires principled action based on abstract concepts tied to reality. Altruism requires Kantian mush, vague, disconnected equivocations, switching contexts, unintelligibility, one reality that is inaccessible by the mind and a second mental universe that is incompetent. Capitalism is a challenge to the individual and it demands his best effort. Altruism demands only envy and hatred of capitalism."[28]

In the book from which the above material was taken, I analyzed the basic premises of both conservatives and progressives. I showed how they both possess the same essential premises. I developed a series of tables which identified some key intellectuals and philosophers of both the left and the right and I exposed the fact that they all advocated altruism. Here is the final chart of this study.

Source	Epistemology	Metaphysics	Ethics/Morality
Father Morris	Faith	God	A Life of Service/Love
Glenn Beck	Faith	Hope	Charity

---

[28] The Conservative's Dilemma by Robert Villegas

George Gilder / Ronald Reagan	Faith	Hope	Love
Georg Hegel	Dialectic	History	Sacrifice
Karl Marx	Historical Materialism	Prosperity	Socialism / Communism
Barack Obama	Faith	Hope	Charity/Sacrifice
Radical for Capitalism / Founding Fathers / Objectivism	Reason	Political Freedom / Rational Egoism / Hope	The Pursuit of Happiness

I also wrote in this book:

"Certainly, the detractors of capitalism have a massive blind spot. Their altruistic premises color their interpretation of historical facts to such a degree that they believe reality conforms to their views. But the defenders of capitalism have a more devastating, yet hardly noticed, blind spot. Their evasion of the evil of altruism has kept them from discovering that capitalism is *the* moral system--the system to be advocated with fire and vigor and enthusiasm. It is, after all, freedom among men that makes capitalism successful. It is the possibility of moral living that makes capitalism the moral system.

"The idea that liberated our country is that no man should live as a serf. This idea created the most successful nation in the history of the planet. Freedom is what makes America a better place to live. Freedom is what makes Americans the happiest and most tolerant people on this earth. Freedom is what makes us the envy of the world. Freedom is what makes us hated, not because we are decadent, but because, as a nation, we give every citizen the possibility of creating his own happiness by means of his own thought. We are the first nation since the Greeks that made moral living possible on earth.

"The mortal enemies of freedom are those who believe that men are moral only when they perform ritual sacrifice. Freedom is the enemy of the man who believes deep down in the core of his being that if men were free, *he* would not be able to survive.

"Are most intellectuals and economists biased against capitalism? Yes, as long as they hold that altruistic self-sacrifice is the proper morality for man and for an economic system. Are they right? No, and no amount of condescending argument that says capitalism will achieve the goals of altruists will work against intellectuals who hate themselves and men. No amount of cheery debate against people that want slavery for men will enable capitalism to win. The haters of capitalism must be exposed as haters of men and haters of freedom.

"We must fight for capitalism based upon man's right to be free, his right to property, his right to speak and think and his right to happiness. Consequences, such as the fact that capitalism creates the most vibrant economy, are irrelevant. Capitalism is moral because only free men can be moral."[29]

---

[29] The Conservative's Dilemma by Robert Villegas

Beginning to Argue for Capitalism

In a previous chapter, "Is Capitalism Moral?", I offered a number of critical economic factors that influence the functioning of a "capitalist system". Each of these factors represents an economic principle that liberates individual choice in a number of critical ways. The basic argument for laissez faire capitalism is that freedom brings about efficient trade because it enables moral living – people are free to make all of the decisions about their lives and this liberates the reasoning mind to tackle the problem of living well. The so-called "greater good" is therefore a false promise. No good can come about when people are interfered with in their consensual activities.

Yet, today, in the name of the greater good, government declares its right to interfere with free trade. They corrupt the concept of justice by claiming to restrict unfair treatment of people. The government declares, in essence, that by restricting free trade, it is thwarting capitalist exploitation. What it is doing is restricting the moral actions of people and destroying their affluence.

What they ignore is that freely chosen transactions among individuals are based upon the rational self-interest of the trading parties. This gets to the heart of the motivation behind the idea of restricting free trade; anti-capitalists want to keep you from pursuing your happiness. They would rather that you be a slave who does what he is told rather than a free person responsible for his own wellbeing. They think that the "greater good" can only be accomplished when government technocrats tell you what to do.

This "greater good" argument is often called the utilitarian argument – but there is a better argument that has scarcely been considered by the defenders of capitalism, many of whom are themselves the worst defenders of freedom (as we saw above). It is the moral argument which holds that restricting free choice is immoral, and more, enabling free choice liberates moral action. This argument holds that capitalism is history's only moral economic system because it leaves people free. In his lecture series, Capitalism: The System of the Mind, Andrew Bernstein tells us:

"Todays' capitalist and semi-capitalist nations are the freest and by far the most prosperous countries on earth. The non-capitalist nations by contrast lack both freedom and prosperity. Despite these widely acknowledge facts there is wide-spread hostility toward capitalism among contemporary intellectuals, journalists and politicians. To protect our rights and our hard-earned wealth, we need to understand the full glories of capitalism, including its history, and then stand up for it with the proud certainty that comes only from comprehensive knowledge of the subject."[30]

Bernstein implies that, in the field of human action, there is a connection between prosperity and free choice. Capitalism produces better results (than any

---

[30] Capitalism: the System of the Mind, lecture course by Andrew Bernstein. ARI (Ayn Rand Institute)

other system) because prosperity is tied to freedom of the mind and reason. Capitalism enables the human mind and this enables the individual to act in such a way that his choices, his purchases, his productive decisions lead to a better life.

Needless to say, today's socialist thinks free choice for the individual is all wrong, backwards. He already "knows" that capitalism is evil because it enables profit. But it is the socialist's Medieval view of profit that is backward. They would rather outlaw profit because it represents a promise of a better life for the individual as opposed to the elites who have captured his mind using altruistic appeals. For these Medievalists, profit is evil because it enables the individual to keep the surplus between his costs and his expenditures. To them his profits belong to the collective and they declare themselves the enforcers of the collective good. What gives them that status? The fact that they don't produce and that whatever they think they know is somehow right? If they teach us to ask "how do you know that you know?", then why can't we ask them "how do you know that you know we don't know?" ad infinitum.

The difference between capitalism and socialism can be found in analyzing the attitude each system has about the individual and his rights. Capitalism holds that the individual should be able to make a profit through his or her honest work, and that making a profit is the essence of living a moral life. A person should be proud of his profits and he or she should guard them and keep them.

Socialism and all other coercive systems, hold that the individual is a member of a collective and that the rights of the collective supercede those of the individual. If the collective, through the government, wants to take the profits of the individual for the sake of the collective, it is denying to the individual his right to live his own life.

Yet, many people, because these ideas have been preached to us since we were children, innocently think that there is some validity to the collective argument and some meekly say, "ok" and agree to give up our most precious values because they tell us it is the right thing. What if we ask them to prove that they have a right to what we earn? What is their definition of "right" and how does it validate their arbitrary confiscations for the sake of the group? The fact is, the can only get away with it because they are more in number than you. What if you challenge their "right" and say, "I won't give them up." "You can't take them."

If individuals are allowed to keep their production, and to trade them as they see fit, the vast majority of individuals will make the right decisions for themselves and their families. They will engage with each other profitably, meaning that their trades, for the most part, will be mutually beneficial. This factor justifies the theoretical framework that creates a dynamic society in which trade, quality and change add up to ever-improving living standards. Society, as a whole, will become richer and more productive. In other words, society will actually be better for people if people do not think collectively and self-sacrificially. If people use their minds to decide what is in their self-interest, they will conclude that trade, cooperation, property rights and individual rights are the way to improve society; not confiscation, commands, collective ownership and nihilism.

One critical factor that I discussed in the first chapter was the fact that, in a capitalist system, because the individual keeps his production and profit, it is possible for men to accumulate large amounts of capital. If that capital is allowed to grow, meaning if the individual is allowed to keep his profit, a system develops wherein the cost of production is cycled through each stage of production (investment, property acquisition, production, sale, delivery and then re-investment) repeatedly while the profits, the difference between the cost of production and the price of the product, is used by the producer as he sees fit. He can enjoy his life with it or invest part of the profits into diversified investments, product research and new businesses. If this process is allowed to continue, society becomes ever more advanced and affluent. I call it the social safety net of capitalism.

Let's set the intellectual foundations for a capitalist mindset:

The Fallacy of Technocracy

Under socialism, the individual's surplus production is considered property of the state. This destroys the incentive for the individual to be productive and he will pursue, over time, bare subsistence instead of profits. Additionally, if politicians siphon off profits for their own uses, then individuals and societies are impoverished over time and living standards are marginally reduced. The society, under socialism, will be corrupt and immoral because it forbids morality to the individual.

Socialists think capitalism is not the most advanced and successful system in history. They think there must be something wrong with it because it is based upon individualism rather than collectivism. For them, capitalism is immoral because the individual thinks of himself first. Prosperity, they think must proceed from the collective and its good management of society. By collecting the profits of the workers, the state thinks it can progressively improve society as more and more money is collected. They think the government's role is to make men sacrifice efficiently. They ask, how can theft and profits under capitalism lead to a better economy when the individual is allowed to waste them on himself? If one party loses in every transaction, is this not evil?

So, the socialist argues that an advanced economic system is made possible by the machines that produce so much – not by the desire for profits. What society needs, they think, are competent technocrats who have the knowledge and intelligence necessary to marshall human action and steer it toward production and affluence that the government can use to improve society. Government knows best, they think.

Technocracy, however, is a dead end. No one is smart enough to know how to coerce the thousands and thousands of economic decisions made on any given day. This has been proven by virtually every communist and socialist experiment in history starting with the Soviet Union, communist China and, today, Venezuela. Whenever a "great" socialist leader decides he knows how to run the energy industry of a country, for instance, he winds up making the decisions *for* the marketplace and, he winds up deciding all aspects of the process, investment, capitalization, real estate, capital equipment, labor, production, package, marketing, logistics and money transactions. Ostensibly, the government benevolence that makes all these decisions is intended to improve the lives of the people; but because there is no self-interest in a society where one man makes all the decisions, people stop thinking for themselves and, over time, they stop being productive. Everything stagnates. They become the slaves of the technocrats and the last consideration is whether they are happy or living well. What is missed is that they can never be happy if all decisions are made for them. They can only be mindless dupes performing robotic movements and doing as they are told.

In fact, socialist technocrats have never proven they have the intelligence to replace the economic decisions of millions of individuals over the course of a single day, let alone over the course of decades. And with all these people relying on the decisions of technocrats what happens when the main technocrat dies or decides to take a vacation? Must everything stop until he is replaced?

Truly, no one could be that smart anyway and, in fact, every individual who is allowed to make his own rational decisions, is smarter than the technocrat. This is because the technocrat decides for groups, not for individuals and the individual, left to his own devices, knows much more about himself, his needs, his feelings than any technocrat who decides for him can possibly know. If some individuals must suffer when the technocrat makes a collective decision, the individual must be sacrificed, especially if he is nameless and can be ignored in press releases. The technocrat promises that thousands of people will be benefited by his decrees but does not mention the many who will have to give up their values for the sake of the group. In many cases, these technocrats know that many people will suffer from the government's coercive measures.

The Fallacy of Scarcity

The zero-sum view of the anti-capitalist medievalists comes from an even older idea that derived from tribalism; that is the view that living in society is about eking out survival in a world of scarcity.

In a world of scarcity, man has to literally scratch the earth to find even the smallest edible food or usable relic. In this world, man is reduced to a position of foraging on an essentially barren planet. Because of this presumed scarcity, men can only subsist, do their best in a bad situation; always live hand to mouth, so to speak. There is no such thing as abundance in this world; life is only about foraging in a desert. This makes survival a competition among individuals to get whatever they can before other men get it.

The idea of a world of scarcity is a cognitive error of the anti-capitalists. It might have been true for primitive man at a time when he had not known how to make tools; long, long ago, but it is not true since man began to hunt, grow food and make tools. Prosperity became a matter of arranging the natural environment so man could create abundance and make life more enjoyable. It stopped becoming a world of scarcity once man's mind was given the freedom to "exploit" the environment, plant seeds and domesticate animals for the future. Once man began to "develop" his environment, foraging was eliminated and abundance was the order of the day. In a world in which production was possible, trade could be a win/win not a win/lose proposition. These ideas of production and trade made capitalism possible and liberated the human mind for moral living.

But the socialists, being medievalists, think that nature hasn't changed. They think it is still barren and devoid of life, that man should root out the scraps and try to survive any way he can. His perspective on man is that he is a loser, a person who barely gets by. He sees successful people, made possible by capitalism and declares that they should be forced to sacrifice their abundance for the sake of the people who barely know how to survive. If he sees a shoot of green in the distance and some other man from another tribe gets there first, well, he thinks, that means a regrettable fight to the death. The survival of the fittest. That is a zero-sum world.

Life as Conflict

What the medieval altruist sees is a world of conflict. He is oblivious to the idea of man using his mind to "develop" his environment for survival. When a man finds a shoot of green in the desert and plants it in the ground near his home; when he salvages the seeds and saves them in a safe place; he has created an environment where abundance is possible. That is the difference man's mind makes. Socialists have missed the importance of knowledge and long-range planning and are still chained to old wives' tales.

The medievalist thinks that life is conflict. If I find a carrot, it is taken away from the person who didn't find it so, therefore, the winner of that carrot is the man who wrested it from the other. Life is conflict and from this conclusion they jump to the idea that capitalism is not only conflict, it is theft, politics, robbery. They think that production and force are the same thing and that whatever can be "fixed" in this type of society, well, it will take force to ensure that the winners of conflict do not overrun the losers. This is how life is, they think. Regrettably, the medievalist thinks, some people don't sacrifice for others; they are thieves, takers and charlatans; especially evil are the men who harness the productive abilities of people for their own sakes. Such men make slaves of others and reap the rewards while the others are left with starvation wages. These are the capitalists, they tell us.

They say capitalism is exploitation; in fact, it is the answer to exploitation. How could a system that enables each individual to pursue his own happiness be immoral? It is the prerequisite of morality. If most citizens in society achieve their values by their own personal choices, isn't that what it means to have a moral system? Aren't production and the pursuit of happiness moral? If most businesses, in pursuit of profit, provide products and services that improve their customers' lives, isn't that moral? I'm referring to the overwhelming number of business trades that happen every hour of every day in the millions upon millions. These are a result of voluntary trade, not conflict among individuals. In fact, the countless lives that have been improved by capitalism are a clear indication that capitalism is moral and not predatory.

What do the anti-capitalists mean when they say that capitalism is fraught with monopolies and inefficiencies; and that capitalists are always seeking to corner their markets by predatory means such as the use of government to harm competitors. You may be surprised to learn that this so-called "feature" of capitalism, the pursuit of monopoly status, is a characteristic, not of capitalism, but of socialism. It is socialism that requires monopolies and government control. It is socialism that requires the centralized state and government-approved monopolies.

It is typical that a socialist (government appointed) plant manager would ask the government to declare his company to be in the interest of society. It was thought wasteful to have resources wasted by several companies making the same types of products when so much money could be saved by society having one company produce those products. This became especially important in major industries such as energy, agriculture and heavy equipment manufacture that are taken over by technocrats for "the sake of the whole". This is why and how socialism destroyed Venezuela.

In the Soviet Union, as communism developed, men who headed up industries, known as commissars, functioned more like oligarchs and used the power of the state to finance their industries. They sought to ensure that no one else was allowed to provide similar products or services. The result was neither efficiency nor affluence. Because production was controlled by government, particularly prices, product development and quality floundered and markets fell apart. Without a pricing mechanism and the profit motive, socialist businesses could not calculate production goals, costs or prices. They necessarily became inefficient, lost money and could only be supported by government which subsidized their losses and propagandized about non-existent economic prosperity.

Even in our mixed economy, which is not full capitalism, businesspeople with political pull, use government to subsidize different business projects. Because of their knowledge of their industry, they are often asked by government to help write legislation for the industry as a whole. This gives them great power and lots of government contracts. The General Electric Company is one such company whose revenues include significant business done with the government. Such companies tout what they call the government/business alliance which is a form of fascism and government control of the economy. This makes corporations into proxies for the government and forces them to advance the interests of the government in order to gain contracts. A case in point is the Business Roundtable that declared in 2019 that 80 of our countries top corporations will focus on "social justice" rather than shareholder value.

But in a capitalist system, properly, no business gets special treatment from the government and must compete successfully or die[31]. In fact, by definition, if a society allows government interference in the economy, it is no longer capitalist but socialist. This fact is little known even today and many people find themselves defending a mixed system of freedom and force and still calling it capitalism. Ours is a mixed economy and not a capitalist economy. To blame government corruption and economic inefficiencies, perpetrated by government interference, on capitalism is incorrect. Any flaw that results from the government interfering in what would otherwise be free trades should be laid at the hands of socialism and not capitalism.

---

[31] I know this term sounds terminal but people don't actually die when a company goes bust. The company dies so capital resources can be applied to better projects. That means a better future for employees since they are more secure in their jobs now that resources are being used wisely.

People often say that socialism is a moral economic system because it requires that the individual sacrifice for the collective. The idea here is that sacrifice for others is a moral act. What is missed here is that sacrifice of values for the sake of others is a true sacrifice; it means giving up a value that you thought so valuable that you were willing to spend time, energy and intelligence to create; and then you are asked to give it up – how could that be good?

This argument that sacrifice is good also admonishes the advocates of capitalism for their adherence to the idea of self-interest as a motive for action. But it is precisely the morality of altruism that makes socialism and its derivative sytems, including the mixed economy, unworkable, conflict-ridden and harmful to individuals who must give up their production and property. It is this act of confiscation by government that is evil. It is this act of theft that causes all such anti-capitalist systems to fail.

The Fallacy of Social Justice

Additionally, advocates for socialism seldom mention the oppressive nature of government force. They prefer to focus only on the "help" that re-distribution, welfare, government regulations and other coercive mandates provide while they ignore the harm done to the individual producer and capitalist. They use collectivist arguments, altruism and utilitarianism to justify their expropriations. They call the goal of socialism "social justice", which is a misnomer.

Altruism, self-sacrifice, is the fundamental principle of socialism and that means *forced* sacrifice. This idea has been sold as benevolent, noble and good when in fact it results in harm to the productive citizen who is forced to give up his values. This moral atrocity has escaped scrutiny in spite of the fact that it means coercion and force against productive individuals.

Government should never be allowed to use force against honest citizens who are merely trying to live. This should apply to every form of government interference in the economy. The fact that government uses force against individuals is the reason why socialism and all other forms of statism are evil. As long as socialists are able to pretend to be doing the "moral" thing in achieving "social justice", the world will be confronted by the scourge of force, vice, corruption, injustice and death that always comes from the idea of "from each according to his abilities and to each according to his needs". This idea is the source of human evil and directly connected to socialism and the idea that the individual is owned by society.

Like true pragmatists, socialists and progressives think that a certain amount of force actually does good and they seek to define which coercive acts will create the most good. They are oblivious to the fact that force restricts free action; in other words, force is evil and can have no positive benefit. It should be the singular focus of what should be outlawed if we are to have a free and peaceful society. Government should be constitutionally prohibited from violating individual rights and the use of force in economic policy is a violation of individual rights.

The Appeal of Socialism Among the Young

Why does socialism appeal to so many young people? It is the propaganda of altruism, the idea that self-sacrifice is a noble thing, that attracts young people to socialism. Socialism does not, in fact, promise a better world; it promises a moral world, a world where self-interest is outlawed and people spend their time living for others above all other considerations.

Young people think they are thoroughly modern; that they are the best generation in history because they are better educated, know how to use technology and, more importantly, care for their fellow men. They see their parents and previous generations as primitive and selfish, unwilling to sacrifice for their fellow man. And that's it. They have no better argument for the viability of socialism; they only think they will do sacrifice better than their parents.

What they don't know is that the idea of self-sacrifice is one of the oldest ideas in the history of mankind. In fact, countless generations for thousands of years have grappled with their desire to sacrifice for god and society. There is nothing new under the sun when it comes to the idea of sacrifice. Yet, in a very real sense, their parents are wiser. Their parents have lived and seen that life cannot be all sacrifice. In fact, it is impossible to do sacrifice completely and this is a fact, not a moral blot on past generations.

Young people have been indoctrinated since early childhood about the imperative that they should sacrifice for others. Because they are young, they take morality seriously but, unfortunately, they do it without question. It does not take a lot of sophistication to refuse to question a folly. They are not aware that there is no connection between sacrifice and good in society.

Not only does the idea of sacrifice animate the socialist idea, but it also is a religious principle – which means that those young people indoctrinated into socialism are also taught that the "selfishness" of the capitalist ideal is evil and must be fought by any means necessary. Many of them think that if they are going to live their noble ideal, they must destroy all vestiges of capitalism and individualism in society. The result is that young people will vote for socialists who promise to make the altruist ideal mandatory.

Certainly, their teachers are convincing them that altruism is the proper moral philosophy and that the goal of "social democracy" can be established through taxing the rich and regulating capitalism much more strenuously. These "socialists" are essentially pragmatist technocrats who see socialism as an effective system that will bring prosperity. However, their pragmatic philosophy cannot work despite the tremendous appeal of the idea of helping others with other peoples' money.

It is thought part of being a citizen to favor this policy. You do it because you love humanity. They couldn't be more wrong.

Today, the talking heads tell us that "being smart" is about using government force effectively to accomplish an economic result. They neglect the fact that force is a negative; it has negative results and no economic benefit. This makes them the biggest and most stupid of risk takers in history. They have no idea whether collective sacrifice will actually create collective benefits.

Beyond this, there is the fact that today's government bureacrats have never actually had to balance budgets, make payrolls and create products that people want to buy. They have never had to perform their work to the best of their abilities – all of which must be done to the highest level in a competitive market – it is easy for them to come up with "obvious" ideas that are not obvious to someone who has had to actually work to the best of his or her ability.

We are often consoled by the slogan that says, "I was a socialist when I was in college and became a conservative when I got a job and had a family." Some would call this person a sellout, but the truth is that he is merely recognizing the fact that in order to have a good life he must produce and in order to have a very good life, he must produce abundance and invest it wisely.

Capitalism is the only system that operates according to the principle that rewards those who earn more than they consume. Capitalism is the just and moral society because it prohibits governmental interference in the lives of individuals and business organizations. Capitalism rewards those who produce abundance. That is why capitalism is moral and that is why capitalism offers a true social safety net that cannot fail.

The Social Safety Net of Capitalism

When I use the term "social safety net of capitalism", I am not writing about government programs designed to help people when they are unemployed or sick. I am writing about the value that capitalism adds to our lives as long as it is allowed to function freely. As examples, consider the benefits of the following aspects of capitalism:

1. When capital is allowed to accumulate in capitalism, it means bigger, more efficient businesses that are able to obtain the capital necessary for more production. Larger companies means that products and services can be more effectively delivered to customers. This is a benefit to virtually everyone in society whose lives are immeasurably improved.

2. Mass production makes possible the cost savings that enable us to have expensive products such as automobiles, ventilators, hospital beds while also reducing the costs of those products bringing them within the budgets of people with modest incomes. This means you and I can have an automobile and other

(otherwise expensive) products and pay for them from our weekly incomes.

3. The law of supply and demand is a result of a free market where prices are dependent upon the interplay between supply and demand. In a free market prices are dependent upon the calculation by sellers using data received from producers and customers. The law of supply and demand means you pay a price that you are willing to pay without someone arbitrarily raising or lowering it without notice.

4. Corporations functioning as if they were free individuals enable the creation of large groups working cooperatively. These "departments" work efficiently to accomplish complex tasks with effective cost controls. This also helps lower prices and increases production of needed products.

5. A stable currency based upon the value of a rare commodity such as gold creates a stable economy. A stable currency prevents theft through inflation (printing money) and ensures you are not wiped out by a government scheme to launder vast amounts of money and buy votes.

Laissez nous Faire "Leave us Alone"

A major flaw in today's government is that most technocrats think re-distribution actually works. The truth is that it leaves producers defeated in the face of a world that has enacted retribution against them for their success. What the government refuses to acknowledge is that they will always need the dreadful deplorables to keep working if they are to continue their plundering. They must forever pander to them and fake their admiration for them. They may not care what happens to them but they must pretend to care.

It can be argued that there is a "subconscious" diminishment of production among those whose incomes are expropriated by the government. These people may continue working but the loss of incentive is psychologically inevitable and unavoidable. This supports the view that the problems that government seeks to solve through re-distribution are actually created by government in the first place. If the government were to exit the situation long-term, the incentive to produce would resume and prosperity would return. It is strange that no one has noticed this and verified it to offer proof that re-distribution is actually the problem not the solution.

Arguments that say the rich are supported by the rest of society, that there is an implicit "social contract" that requires them to "give back" to society and that they should want to contribute to society by paying higher taxes (while also being denigrated as greedy cut throats) are nothing more than utter cruelty imposed upon 'the rich'. Yet, there are studies which indicate that the wealthy are more "giving" and "considerate" to others than are the leftist re-distributors in society.

If you really want validation of the idea that the left is destroying our prosperity, all you have to do is listen to them and you'll hear the undertone of envy and hatred toward success in society. The Elizabeth Warrens and Bernie Sanders and AOCs of the current crop are dreadful people who should be fired for what they are doing to our country.

All dictatorships are re-distribution schemes. Fascism is the redistribution of wealth from productive property owners to the government and special interests. Socialism is a more advanced form of fascism where the government controls the major industries in order to accomplish the same goals. Welfare-statism is the focus of government on re-distributing income from the wealthy to the non-working poor. Communism is the re-distribution of property once owned by a propertied "class" and the taking of that property by a government elite (presumably) for the sake of workers who are a proxy for government elites.

All these schemes result in the expropriation or theft of productive power by political power. There is no need to talk about which system is better, which allocates funds better; they are all the same in that they use force against productive citizens to the detriment of those people. All types of re-distribution hurt people regardless of effort. Once re-distribution takes hold, the ablest people will slow their effort because they know their product will be given to others. On the other hand, the less able will also slow their effort because they too know the government will re-distribute their effort.

This means that all effort, over time, is reduced and the system becomes finger pointing and bickering about who is working hard enough to support the group. This is why no socialist system ever works; why most of them fail and end with bloodshed. Re-distribution is theft of property and energy and because so it reduces both the amount of property created and the effort required to produce it. It is a historically proven fact that whenever you establish re-distribution, your nation is on the path toward destruction.

The productive individual is the most important citizen in our economy, not because he or she spends money from a printing press but because he or she makes things that can be traded; things that make life better for others who buy them. It is the productive citizen who is exploited in a mixed or socialist economy.

If we are going to have a viable movement for individual rights in America, then it must be a philosophical movement. It must be a movement of ideas that recognizes the clear differences between the productive citizen and the looters in the government. The individual must educate himself on the reasons why we originally had a free society, on the genius of the principles elaborated in the Constitution and why they are the only hope for humanity. It means recognizing that the individual has a pivotal role in saving his country and defeating the enemies of freedom. It means you stand for the Constitution and especially for capitalism as the expression of freedom, property and capital savings which are the pillars of an affluent and happy society. But it also means that you control the government; you limit its powers and whenever it becomes predatory and coercive, you refuse to participate in the looting and refuse to be looted.

It is inconsistent for the individual to accept one form of re-distribution against others while being against only those forms that affect him directly. If you disapprove of having your own money re-distributed, you should be against all re-distribution. Below are the various forms of re-distribution in our society:

- Economic regulation of businesses re-distributes market share to businesses favored by government
- Taxes re-distribute money from the most productive citizens to the less productive
- Government ownership of businesses re-distributes jobs, income and profits to bureaucrats and favored labor unions
- Welfare programs such as direct payments to "the poor" re-distribute income from those better able to use property to those who can't manage their money
- Government management of industries provides jobs for government appointees and siphons

profits to party campaign committees (Fannie Mae and Freddie Mac)
- Government regulations created sub-prime mortgages which re-distribute loans from people with good credit ratings to people who are credit risks – this creates a massive shift of capital from productive banking activities to worthless packaged securities, shifting huge amounts from insurance companies and government to banks that had thought the securities were backed by the government - resulting in re-distribution of half of the value in the stock market and almost half of the value in 401Ks from American savers to short sellers
- TARP gives taxpayer dollars to banks that don't need it or that should go out of business
- Stimulus programs re-distribute taxpayer income to government social engineering programs
- Tariffs restrict international commerce and destroy jobs
- Onerous immigration regulations keep freedom-loving people from being "legal" and reduces the pool of needed and low-wage workers
- Laws favor unions over employers, creating unnecessary dues-paying jobs, forcing employers to pay workers too much, destroying the work ethic and raising prices while also sending businesses overseas
- Government education of our children indoctrinates them for collectivism before it teaches them viable job skills, and

- Any scheme that involves the use of tax money for anything other than police, courts and military defense re-distributes safety from the law-abiding citizen to the criminal
- Altruism of any kind practiced by government re-distributes moral action and gives the result to people who do not practice moral behavior

In order to have peace and security, arbitrariness must be removed from the actions of government. The government should never be allowed to interfere in the private business of citizens. Lawfulness means treating all citizens equally and without caprice; it means having a respect for property rights. A proper government recognizes that the principles of re-distribution and expropriation are violent acts and the government which engages in them does not deserve to govern. A bad law is no law at all among free people.

A market society provides the framework for efficient commerce. As we read before, capitalism makes it possible for enterprising individuals to practice a series of principles that are based upon individual rights. When property is left in the hands of those who are able to use it; all citizens benefit – rich and poor alike. The rich provide factories that produce life-serving products. They also provide jobs and better lives for the formerly poor who are given an opportunity to earn their livelihoods, to gain property, even to become rich themselves and to enjoy life. This has always been the outcome when a society is left free.

The idea that capitalism exploits the poor and keeps them poor is a lie. All you need to do is observe the actions of a capitalist and you'll learn that his focus is not on taking from the poor but providing products and services to productive people which gives the poor an opportunity to join the ranks of the productive. Government coercion, on the other hand, exploits both rich and poor and reduces them to bare subsistence.

The poor today were not made poor by capitalism; they were made poor by government; by the principle of redistribution which removed investment capital from producers and diverted it to consumption. The negative impact on jobs and opportunity in the economy, over time, is palpable.

The proper principle for a good society is that of "Laissez Faire" which means that the government should be "hands off" when it comes to the economic lives of citizens. This means that government cannot be allowed to enact legislation that interferes in the lives and decisions of citizens.

Capitalism, the Perfect System

"The best way to understand a historical phenomenon is to start at the beginning and examine the causal factors that gave rise to it. Prior to the capitalist revolution of the 18th century, Fuedalism and its legacy dominated Europe. Fuedalism, the ancient regime, was the dictatorship of the hereditary aristocracy. Millions of commoners, who made up the overwhelming preponderance of mankind, were subordinated to the dictates of kings, lesser nobles and the Church. For centuries, serfs were tied to the land and commoners, more broadly, had no rights. The dominant economics of the period was some variant of mercantilism, a direct application of the dictatorship of the aristocracy. Wealth was construed as bullion in the national treasury which was used to finance the wars of kings and wealth emphatically was not conceived as the wide-spread availability of consumer goods and services that raised man's general standard of living. The king and his aristocratic advisers controlled the economy and intervened regularly to levy taxes, to establish guilds and apprenticeships, to ban a free labor market, to impose tariffs and prohibit free trade, etc.

"If you seek to understand the essence of an age, go to its fundamentals. Since the mind is mankind's survival instrument, ask the question, what was the period's characteristic attitude towards the mind? During the pre-capitalist feudal era, the answer to that question was not a happy one. The dominant philosophy came from Christianity which stipulated faith over reason. Politically, the aristocrats tolerated no intellectual criticism of their rule. The free thinking mind was proscribed by both state and church. The result of course was brutal oppression. During the dark and middle ages, for example, heretics of a dozen varieties, including such serious intellectual challengers as the Pelagians[32] and the Manicheans[33], as well as their later intellectual heirs, were routinely suppressed and often put to death. As late as the 17th century, Giordano Bruno was burned at the stake and Galileo threatened with torture for disagreeing with Church doctrine. Even in the 18th century, Voltaire was confined in the Bastille. Diderot, the editor of and driving force behind the encyclopedia, was imprisoned. Dalembert, the great scientist and writer was intimidated by the authorities into temporarily abandoning his association with the encyclopedia. The crime of each and of many more, similarly punished, was independent thought.

"It would be impossible to calculate how many potential Isaac Newtons, Thomas Edisons et al, were compelled into bondage on the manorial fields over the centuries; or at the very least, stifled by the arbitrary power of the ancient regime. With the best, the most creative minds suppressed, progress was impossible. The result was the most abysmal destitution and misery.

---

[32] Pelagianism is the belief that original sin did not taint human nature and that mortal will is still capable of choosing good or evil without special divine aid. Source: Wikipedia

[33] A dualistic religious system with Christian, Gnostic, and pagan elements, founded in Persia in the 3rd century by Manes (c. 216–c. 276). The system was based on a supposed primeval conflict between light and darkness. It spread widely in the Roman Empire and in Asia, and survived in eastern Turkestan (Xinjiang) until the 13th century. Source: Oxford Dictionary

"There is a myth put forth by the Marxists that the pre-capitalist era was a golden age of the workers and of the non-aristocratic guys working in the domestic industry. Myth is the right term for that; it is an unadulterated falsehood. There is not a shred of historical truth to that.

"Poverty, famine and disease were endemic throughout the feudal era. For example, the bubonic plague wiped out almost one third of Europe's population in the 14th century and recurred incessantly into the 18th as well as many other diseases. Famine too was widespread in Europe until the 18th century killing sizable portions of the population in Scotland, in Finland and Ireland and causing misery and death even in such relatively prosperous countries as England and France.

"Regarding living standards, one economist, Angus Madison, in his book Phases of Capitalist Development,...states that 'economic growth, during the centuries 500 to 1500 was non-existent.' That means, zero, nada, the null set, nothing and that per capital income rose by merely 0.1 percent per year in the years 1500 to 1700. In 1500, Madison estimates, the European per capital GDP was roughly $215. In 1700, roughly $275."[34]

What was the cause of this poverty? Political systems are based on ethical systems. Ethical systems are based upon our view of man as either autonomous or incompetent. If men choose the wrong ethical system,

---

[34] *Capitalism: the System of the Mind*, lecture course by Andrew Bernstein. ARI (Ayn Rand Institute)

then the result will be false choices and false actions that lead to failure. So, which is true, is man autonomous and capable or is he incompetent and incapable?

If you think that man is autonomous, you celebrate his individuality and his nature as a thinking being who is essentially good. You develop an ethical system that honors that nature. If you think man is incompetent, you question his ability to think and understand as well as his ability to choose correct action. You become a critic of man and you seek a society intent on forcing man to take those actions you (or God) deem to be correct.

These are the two choices that lead to two different forms of society. Do you create a society that leaves man free to be his own moral agent; or do you create a society that uses government to ensure he serves the collective? You must select either a free society, limited government, or a dictatorship, unlimited government. These are your only choices.

A limited government, by its nature, creates a capitalist society and the dynamism that comes from independent thought. An unlimited government creates an authoritarian society and the stagnation that comes with having a few people decide for a large number. Although it may be hard for some to accept, a capitalist society unleashes self-interest while an authoritarian society restricts people to sacrifice, altruism and self-denial.

Today, in our society, there is a struggle between these

two systems. We have not made up our minds about our view of man's nature. We have been flailing about, so to speak, and this has created our present situation in which authoritarianism holds sway. The advocates of authoritarianism are now free to move forward to full dictatorship.

The correct decision about the proper society rests on the question of man's method of survival. Man is a creature of a certain type. He survives by means of his mind. He uses reason and knowledge and makes choices based upon his findings. This is the essence of the matter; if you hold that man's mind is sacrosanct, you will favor freedom and self-sufficiency, in short, limited government.

That division between our views of man's means of survival revolves around the question about whether man survives by means of his own mind or the minds of others. My view, my reason for favoring capitalism, is that capitalism is the only economic system that enables man to survive by means of his own mind. If you ask yourself, what should man do in order to survive, the only answer can be that he use his mind, ascertain reality and act to effect his wellbeing.

In truth, man can only survive by means of thinking. If he decides to suspend his mind, the only other way for him to survive is by enslaving the men who think. If we establish a society where dependence leads to survival, then the only result will be devastation.

For instance, we've seen a pervasive negativity expressed toward business in the media and the entertainment arts. Intellectuals, actors and commentators are forever sneering at the giants of industry, who, in their "ruthless" pursuit of profit, supposedly broke laws, cheated consumers, and generally, but successfully, made life miserable for all. Yet, there is very little evidence that the vast majority of "capitalists" are evil people. They were considered such because of their association with self-sufficiency and independence which are assumed by society to be negative traits.

From the philosophical arena we are taught that those who seek self-interest necessarily seek it at the expense of others. Such attitudes toward self-interest reach their lowest point when a President of the United States scorns businessmen for not sacrificing themselves to the inflationary policies of the government (See Kennedy vs. U.S. Steel or Obama vs. just about everybody).

The difference between those who favor authoritarianism and those who favor limited government is that authoritarians are anti-conceptual. They slice reality up into hundreds of out-of-context critiques of capitalism where nothing connects and anything goes. Authoritarians betray a desire to enslave men and put them under their rule. To accomplish this, they take bold leaps into the future and work steadfastly under the belief that the end justifies the means. If one bold leap fails, they never question themselves and their motives; they merely take another bold leap to see if it works.

For instance, an authoritarian develops no universal principles that relate to man except that he is an economic creature. As a child of pragmatism, the authoritarian believes that man is incapable of learning from sense experience and, because so, we can only try different approaches to social organization in order to define those that work. The result is an activist who cannot see the difference between limited government and authoritarianism.

A pragmatist could be a Marxist who sees no connection between one era of history and another. He would say that during an earlier agricultural age, private property developed out of a need to protect crops from being trampled or stolen. According to this view, the idea of property might have been valid in that context, but when industrial society took shape, the idea became obsolete because of the advent of collective rights. There are no principles for a pragmatist.

These varying authoritarian critiques of capitalism create whole new branches of so-called social sciences, with each science taking off in different directions yielding a myriad of conclusions and social engineering schemes. The question is not how to establish a universal principle valid through the ages but how to manipulate one idea for the sake of accomplishing a particular "social good". You could study thousands of books about this and learn nothing more than different ways to coerce men and ruin society.

What you have in these two views (limited government versus authoritarianism) is a battle between two opposing systems of government, one that came out of European intellectual circles and the other out of American circles. One, the European, created dictatorship and the other created the United States of America.

The clash between these two views played out in two different periods; the first during the American Revolutionary War where a free society won; and the other during World War I and World War II where the two sides fought to a virtual stalemate. Although freedom won the wars during the 20th century, the ideas of Europe prevailed and European style totalitarianism is again on the verge of taking over the world. We may soon experience again the devastation that rocked Europe during the last century.

Today, once again, capitalism is under attack. The mixed (economy) forms of capitalism are about to be wiped out and forever disappear. The reason for this is that intellectuals hate the individualism and egoism that are an intricate element of capitalism. The progressives' adherence to the Marxist/authoritarian critique of capitalism, and their hatred of profit, has left capitalism with almost no defense. Few are willing to fight for the right of the individual to be an egoist (especially among CEOs). Yet, that is what it would take for capitalism to be defended.

In practically every discussion of egoism, we hear something like this: "Is it right to seek one's self-interest in disregard for the interests of others?" Yet, this is a loaded question. It is based upon a false premise that I call scarcity metaphysics, the idea that one man's good is another man's harm and that profit is theft. Such a view implies a total ignorance of property rights, and of the fact that what is rightfully owned by one man cannot in any way relate to the wellbeing of another. What one man earns has nothing to do with what any other man earns (or does not earn) for himself.

When Marxists and OWS[35] protestors tell us it is time to ditch capitalism, they want us to believe that capitalism causes harm to man and society. It is this lie about capitalism which must be challenged. Capitalism is a boon to mankind and the cause of all the good done by free economies. We should, instead, ditch socialism and re-distribution for they are the cause of harm to the productive and the good. Indeed, socialism is the criminal system of history, the destroyer of good and abundance. Socialism is the cause of poverty, concentration camps, slavery and hunger.

The idea that those who engage in trade are evil reveals a bias by authoritarians against self-interest and should remove them from serious consideration. These people should be ditched along with socialism, re-distribution and Marxism. That such thinking takes place in view of the obvious evidence against it is another example of

---

[35] Occupy Wall Street

the extent to which the idea of collective sacrifice has corrupted our culture.

Sometimes they tell us: "Complain about socialism all you want, but it won't do the slightest bit of good unless you can persuade have-nots that you have a better alternative for them." What could this possibly mean? That complaining about socialism is somehow wrong-headed? Ask the millions killed by Stalin and Mao and Pol Pot. Did they experience the wonders of socialism? And would they reject capitalism as a false promise when there are so many living under the affluence of nations that have a mere semblance of capitalism? Again, we see an example of the intellectual argument that yields no actual benefit to people. The answer can only be, yes, we will complain about socialism because it is an evil system of slavery and death; and, yes, capitalism is the greatest, most successful economic system ever invented by man. How could anyone doubt this?

One problem with anti-capitalists and their arguments, almost to a man (woman), is that they assume capitalism to be steeped in conflict and contradiction. Perhaps this comes from their childhoods or from their mentors, but for some reason, they project a state of conflict into the very essence of capitalism. They frame all their arguments in terms of opposing forces and then paint themselves as "good" people seeking to defeat the "bad". This is because they do not trust the human mind to correctly ascertain reality and their insecurity makes them want to construct a reality that will never exist; so they pretend to feel good about the false ideas they advocate.

Yet, capitalism is about, indeed requires, principles such as cooperation, good will and a synthesis between the economic demands of consumers and the abilities of need fillers (capitalists). Capitalism enables positive relationships between those willing to buy and those willing and able to sell. This is a peaceful process of value creation, value sales and mutual benefit. No one forces bad products on people (that happens in cronyist systems such as fascism and socialism).

In fact, capitalism is the most efficient system on the planet for matching consumer needs with need fillers. This is because it lets "value production" meet "customer-demand". In a sense, customers are allowed to vote in the free market that counts orders and profits.

In contrast to the cooperation inherent in capitalism, we have the "command" method of controlled economies, where bureaucrats (technocrats) make production decisions and set prices, guessing wrongly about demand, then expropriating funds from tax payers to correct the economic miscalculations they have made.

Capitalism is a value system in which capitalists are free to fill real and immediate demands using their own or borrowed funds. They obtain their reward when the fulfillment of customer needs is achieved. Socialism, the command economy, is inefficient because it is based on bureaucratic decisions that are almost always wrong, too late, aimed at the wrong people and/or corrupt. The result is not success but subsidized loss.

Capitalism is the perfect economic system because it liberates the producer to make what people need. When it does this across a vast economy, the market tips off the capitalist about where to invest for future production. Everyone wins. Contrary to the unfounded criticism of socialists and other progressives, this essential principle known as "freedom in transactions" is all that capitalism is.

The only "exploitation" found in capitalism occurs when someone decides to deceive or otherwise cheat someone in a transaction. The saving feature of capitalism is that a cheater, once discovered, loses customers and goes out of business (or he goes to jail for fraud or some other crime). But this "possibility" of cheating exists to a much higher degree in socialism because the cheater can use the power of government to "get over" on his customers; whereas, in capitalism, he suffers a bad reputation and loss of business.

Needless to say, the leftists are cynical about the mutuality of free trade in capitalism because they are essentially cynical about man, his mind and his ability to survive. This is why they are always finding something in capitalism that "needs to be fixed" by some new (or old) form of government interference in the marketplace. They mistakenly take trade to be a cynical effort to cheat people and declare themselves the only people smart enough to decide how to fix it. This, to them, is the essence of life: cheating; and that makes the only cheaters in the debate over capitalism and socialism to be the socialists. They are cheating man out of his need to survive.

It is socialism that is full of inefficiencies because its goal is not the satisfaction of consumer demand but of invented "social" needs. These "needs" are supposedly fulfilled, under socialism, by unwilling providers and presented in a "take it or leave it" manner with little concern for the desires of the consumer. The only "satisfied" party in a socialist transaction is the central authority.

In order to understand how a proper society should work, we should realize that, in a sense, every man is a Robinson Crusoe. And this fact is what makes every man a capitalist and every capitalist an egoist. Every man must find ever more efficient methods for improving his survival. In the same manner that, for Robinson Crusoe, his goal was a better life on a desert island, for modern man, the goal is a higher standard of living. But like Robinson Crusoe, modern man must find a way to lighten the effort needed for bare survival. He does it through invention and production which create the profit that yields a higher standard of living. If a man's productive efforts yield him more than he needs for bare survival, he can then look around for products that help raise the quality of his life; he creates demands for such products and stimulates their production; he creates a need for advertising and promotion of such products so he can be made aware of what is available.

Somewhere along the way, someone will invent a product that was unthoughtof by many men and this creates new markets and significant advances in the standard of living.

In contrast, the controlled economy is based on consumption only without reference to the votes of the consumers. By destroying property rights, this system thinks it can obtain the results that derive from property rights through a coercive takeover of the factories. Their critique that property rights worked in an agricultural society but are not necessary in an industrial society is the reason they cavalierly dismiss capitalists and expropriate (monopolize) the factories. What they don't understand is that machines don't run themselves, they need human intelligence and a rational goal – and the only person willing to apply his intelligence to machines is the person who has a stake in them, the man who is both owner and genius – a person who cannot survive under socialism because socialism destroys ownership.

Reality tells us that the existence of high capacity machines does not eliminate the need for property rights. In fact, property rights are a concept that recognizes an enduring need of man; that he functions more efficiently when his right to keep what he creates is recognized. Property rights worked in a primitive society of two people five million years ago; they work in an advanced society of millions today and will work on a spaceship in some distant future transporting colonists to a new planet. Property rights do not become obsolete with new machines; they become more necessary as the machines become more advanced. Better machines do not create a need for collectivism; they create a need for ingenuity and innovation in the output of new products.

This means that every man is a businessman and every businessman is a worker: in order to survive, he must produce, and in order to survive well, he must produce more than is necessary for bare subsistence. This law applies all across the economic spectrum from Robinson Crusoe to Bill Gates. To preach that profits are exploitation is not only an attack on disembodied corporations; it is an attack on every person who has a desire for accomplishment.

In a free society, man is not merely chained to bare subsistence. He is also a creature of pleasure who yearns for rest, enjoyment and celebration. He needs to produce more than he consumes because he needs to experience the totality of being human. Only surplus production can make this possible; yet it is this surplus production the authoritative state wants to take away.

By nature, man is an egoist...and this is not a bad thing; it is a quality that makes enjoyment and higher thinking possible. It preaches accomplishment and joy; the value of work and intellect and brings the ability to understand and experience the magnificence of life (and the experience of this wondrous universe). Its hallmark is human value and loving life.

In this wonderful sense, the sense of joy and accomplishment, capitalism cannot exist without the human mind that yearns for the best. Man's mind must be exercised and when capitalism is diminished so is human striving and valuing. Socialists of all varieties are therefore killers of men and society. They are the reason that nations fail while capitalism brings a cycle of excellence in accomplishment.

On the other hand, subsistence economics, the zero-sum economy of socialism, is a scheme to subvert man's happiness, undertaken by those who would dictate his choices and steal the surplus he produces. It is no accident that authoritarians take little consideration of man's ability to choose for himself, and that they preach their theories in the midst of the most technologically advanced economy in human history. They preach it, not despite the greatness of the productive U.S. citizen, but because of it. They have to find a way, through deception, to convince the American citizen that he has the most corrupt system ever devised; not so they can make things better for him but so they can take over his property and especially his machines. It is a conman's game that today's socialists are playing. Like the savages they are, when the machines stop, they'll point their guns at the closest person and tell him to fix the machines or else.

Has capitalism failed?

Hardly. It is socialism that is failing around the world.

Alcoholism and Addiction – the System

These four books comprise a system that can be used by both patients and counselors who are battling Alcoholism and Addiction. Based upon Mr. Villegas's own system developed during his struggle against alcoholism, this system includes:

Alcoholism and Addiction – A Secular Ten-Step Program
This groundbreaking book offers a secular approach to alcoholism unlike that offered by Alcoholics Anonymous. We recommend that every individual going for alcohol and drug-abuse counseling be given a copy of this book which contains the workbook and the two versions of The World's first drunk. http://amzn.to/2md6R9w $3.45 Kindle $11.95 softcover

The Secular Ten-Step Program Workbook
This booklet covers the program developed by Mr. Villegas. It is designed as a workbook with blank spaces for the patient to write his own thoughts as he takes each of the ten steps. Order one copy for each patient in counseling. http://amzn.to/2lrHimS $4.49 Kindle $6.95 softcover

The World's First Drunk – With Counselor Talking Points
This booklet is designed for the counselor as he works with patients during individual or group therapy. It contains helpful tips on discussing the life story of the man who invented alcohol. Order one copy for each patient in counseling. http://amzn.to/2l446Wr $2.99 Kindle $5.95 softcover

The World's First Drunk – Patient Version
This version of the short story contains empty spaces where the patient can answer questions about the life story of the man who invented alcohol. Order one copy for each counselor. http://amzn.to/2ldxBGb $2.99 Kindle $5.95 softcover.

www.robertvillegas.com

Business Books by Robert Villegas

These four books by Robert Villegas comprise some of the business books that he has written. As an executive working for several companies, he was able to develop these methods that will help anyone seeking to excel in the business world. These books are:

How to Be a Great Employee – and a Greater Manager
You cannot be a great manager without first being a great employee. And this is something that requires learning, experience and attitude. The attitude comes from you but the learning and experience you should acquire through diligent study and practice. http://amzn.to/2BqdG2i $3.99 Kindle $8.95 softcover

SWOT Analysis Supercharged
A SWOT Analysis is an objective look at the internal and external elements of your organization that impact your success or lack thereof. If done diligently, you will always have a handle on what you need to do to improve season after season.
http://amzn.to/2BCAWYx $3.99 Kindle $6.95 softcover

The Five-Module Call Center Training System
The Five-Module Call Center Training System is designed to assist the Call Center Team Leader in helping his employees quickly upgrade their skills to an acceptable level. http://amzn.to/2B3Svj1 $3.99 Kindle $5.95 softcover

Website Development Methodology
Effective strategic marketing requires the ability to differentiate the website development organization and its deliverables from those of the competition. http://amzn.to/2DnYMgh $2.99 Kindle $12.95 softcover.

www.robertvillegas.com

The REAL Purpose-Driven Life

The REAL Purpose-Driven Life
After centuries of being told that it is not about you, it is time to set the record straight. You are a unique individual and your goal in life should be to achieve your own happiness.
https://amzn.to/2XyrpPf $3.50 Kindle $7.95 softcover

Values and Purpose Workbook
This book is about you. It's about time. After centuries of being told that nothing is about you, it is time to set the record straight. You are a unique individual and your goal in life should be to achieve your happiness. https://amzn.to/2XwlkTv $3.99 Kindle $8.95 softcover

www.robertvillegas.com

Christianity – A New Perspective on Jesus

These three books are based upon a new perspective on the life and person of Jesus. Based upon a new theory of the story of Jesus as an invention of the Roman Imperial Cult, these books add significant new evidence for this theory.

Unkilling Jesus
Starting with Atwill's Caesar's Messiah theories, this book explores the following questions. How was the story of Jesus's life written? Who was Paul and what was his role in the creation of Christianity? What was his provenance and did he actually meet the resurrected Christ? Who wrote Revelation and what was the document's purpose? Why was Domitian assassinated? Who was Clement and what was the nature of his relationships with Peter and Josephus? Were the Pseudo-Clementine materials really "pseudo"? Why did Saulus attack Justus? How were the gospels written? http://amzn.to/2itMCoO $3.99 Kindle $15.95 softcover

Domitian: The Final Messiah
The central goal of this book is to define the specific themes and concepts that make up Domitian's contribution to Christianity – in a sense, we are defining the specific Domitian overlay to the Christian materials originally developed for Titus. http://amzn.to/2yWMSlx $2.99 Kindle $6.95 softcover

Paul's Agon and the Mystification of History
Paul and Jesus are joined in one important way; the way of a miracle. They met on the road to Damascus while Paul supposedly pursued Christians. Jesus, in a sense, told Paul to get with the program and stop persecuting his people. In this incident, the Bible tells us that Jesus is already dead, and resurrected. This book argues otherwise. http://amzn.to/2zSDsuP $5.99 Kindle $19.95 softcover

www.robertvillegas.com

About Robert Villegas

Robert Villegas is an Arizona Author specializing in fiction, romance, theater and philosophy. He was born in South Texas (Weslaco) but raised in Indiana. He is Hispanic-American but American in every sense of the word. He has spent a lifetime in the business world as a UPS executive and also worked in locations all over the United States and Europe. He is an Army veteran who served as a telecommunications specialist serving in the 7th Infantry Division in Camp Casey, Korea. He was educated in Indiana and earned a Degree through the University of the State of NY (Albany) via an external degree program. He is divorced with three grown children and three grandchildren.

Twitter: @RobertVillega18
Facebook: Robert Villegas
www.robertvillegas.com

DSI Kindle and Print on Demand Publishing Services

The world of publishing has changed forever. New digital technologies have made book publishing and distribution virtually immediate. Authors can now have their books formatted and submitted for production virtually overnight. The world of immediate availability and immediate royalties has become a reality.

Yet, you need not worry over the process of ensuring your book is ready for Kindle and Print on Demand. As an experienced book publisher, you can rely on DSI to get your book ready for Kindle publishing and Create Space production and distribution.

Kindle and Create Space are the Amazon-owned business units that can get your book on their systems in a matter of days. DSI can provide the following services:

- Format your book for Kindle **(starting at $200 depending on the size of the book)**
- Format your book for Create Space print publication **(included in the above price)**
- Upload it to both systems **(No charge)**
- Create a stunning cover design that meets Kindle and Create Space guidelines **($200)**
- Create a stunning Internet landing page where you can send book buyers **(starting at $349)**
- Create profile and cover for your Facebook page **($50)**

- Promote your landing page to the search engines so it can be indexed by Google, Bing and hundreds of other search engines **($120)**

We take most major credit cards for these services. Just think about it; you can be earning royalties on your books in a matter of days. If you'd like to obtain a specific quote for our formatting and publishing services, please contact us at 317-881-3826.

www.documentservicesinternational.com

www.ingramcontent.com/pod-product-compliance
Lightning Source LLC
Chambersburg PA
CBHW070233220526
45465CB00004B/1409